Distance Learning

Lou A. Manning
5426 Havenhill Dr
Columbus, OH 43235

Online Education
The Future Is Now . . .
Second Edition

D1216451

Dr. Gerry L. Bedore

Dr. Marlene R. Bedore

Gerry L. Bedore, Jr.

Online Education:
The Future is Now

Dr. Gerry Bedore,
Dr. Marlene Bedore,
and Gerry Bedore, Jr.

BALANCE IS THE GOAL

Distance Learning Technologies Group ®

www.socratesdltg.com

an imprint of ART Press

Publishers	Arnie Kuenn
	Craig King
Acquisitions	Paul Zagnoni
Managing Editor	Jamie Tillman
Technical Editor	Phil Shanks
Copy Editor	Gerald Mallonee
Satellite Graphic	Erica Rossi

This text was created using Microsoft Word 97. The primary font used is Century Schoolbook.

Academic Research & Technologies
2700 North Central, 9th Floor
Phoenix, Arizona 85004
602.266.8530 ◆ FAX 602.266.6404
www.artedu.com

ISBN 1-58176-046-9
Academic Research & Technologies

Table of Contents

Preface

This book is a work in progress. The rate at which distance learning programs are progressing will soon create the need for additional chapters and subjects, so our first revision will be under way about the same time this one reaches the distribution points. This is exciting but at the same time frustrating, because so much more always needs to be said.

The second edition coming forth only one year later validates our observation regarding a work in progress. We will keep the remainder of this front piece intact and note that it is STILL a work in progress. Also please note the addition near the end of this preface - "And Now It Is A Year Later..."

The adventure begins....

Our adventure with online education began in the mid-1980s when, in a conversation with one of the key curriculum people at the University of Phoenix, Terri Hedegaard, the thought of a computer-based online learning paradigm was put on paper. In just a few months, we had a pilot program under way, and before the pilot was complete, we were in production. Today, Terri still leads one of the premier online degree programs in the world from her San Francisco office. She provided the forum for the founder of Socrates Distance Learning Technology Group with the steering committee to pioneer many of the online concepts that are the underpinnings of the programs of today.

The earliest programs used simple shareware bulletin board software technologies to move materials between teachers and students. That was the only technology available for file transfers and dialogue scenarios at the time. The curriculum was directly translated from proven on-ground courses. The only changes were to make the curriculum work online. The first students were randomly selected pioneers, who indicated a willingness to be flexible and tolerant as we launched this new venture. In just a year and a half, the first students graduated from the program, and several other classes had already begun. The program ultimately was submitted to the North Central Association for accreditation and was accepted with enthusiasm by this prestigious group.

And continues….

Since this beginning, many things have changed, but the core concepts used at that time are still valid and operable in several programs. Technologies have improved dramatically with software produced specifically to meet the needs of students in the online environment. With the availability of the Internet, additional options for delivering curricula are becoming available nearly every month. The need for a convenient way for busy people to meet their educational growth needs has fueled the growth of this form of educational delivery. Quality has steadily improved and

acceptance of the education derived from such programs is gaining in academic and business communities daily as graduates contribute in their workplaces.

As online offerings expand, so does the need for qualified people to plan, implement, operate, and teach online programs. Severe shortages exist in all categories at this time. While working with the UCLA Extension (UNEX) program to introduce online delivery to their special educational offerings, a program was proposed to train people to create new online programs. This certificate program, the Certificate of Completion in Online Teaching, is offered online through UNEX and is very popular, particularly among teachers and educational administrators, who have indicated that their schools will pursue online offerings within one to three years.

As we developed and tested curricula for one of the courses in the UNEX certificate program, we discovered that text materials are limited in this area of study. Thus the idea for this book was formed. Like much of the online program, we created as we moved forward.

The material for this book is a compendium of research, ideas, and proven concepts derived from experience in implementing and operating several programs, input from students, and extensive interviewing and discussions of online concepts with experts in this emerging field.

As we developed this material, we thought it would be of value to those who put together programs over the next several years. While details are limited, the charts and diagrams included offer an approach to thinking about a program, evaluating the need, defining the process for implementation and operation, and developing plans for the technology base. We hope you will find this useful as a primer to use in developing your own online programs. Look for revisions and additions as new concepts and options become available.

And now it is a year later...

It was one year ago that the initial copies of this book were given to the first class of students working on a certificate program. We then incorporated the book into a number of training programs for online instructors. Since that time, we have worked with hundreds of students, teachers, trainers, and administrators who are developing, implementing and operating successful programs throughout the United States. The book has proven of great value in supporting our efforts to assist those involved in this exciting opportunity to offer quality education and training programs to the increasing population that find it difficult to attend on-ground classes.

In this year, we have had the opportunity to work with many individuals and institutions in applying the concepts offered in this book to emerging programs. This has reinforced our commitment to the concepts and methods described on the following pages. At the same time, we have been able to observe several programs that were delayed or abandoned. These programs have commonalties that reinforce some of the key messages in this book. We would like to add the following thoughts for your consideration as you approach the contents of this book and consider online programs for your institution.

1. Online programs are NOT intended to replace on-ground programs. Online programs have unique characteristics that allow an institution or a business to reach potential students that cannot attend on-ground classes. Online provides a way to offer quality education in an alternative format where circumstances

indicate a need - they are intended to supplement on-ground programs - not replace them.

2. A substantial investment is required UP-FRONT to develop and implement a successful online program. Institutions that are not ready to make this up-front investment in human and support resources, dollars, and cultural changes, should reconsider pursuing a program. Program proposals should be subjected to the scrutiny of financial, cultural, and mission checks just as with any business decision. Online programs are not ways to instantly increase enrollment or cash-flows - they will provide opportunities for meaningful growth if properly planned, funded, and implemented.

3. Resistance to the changes required for implementing a successful online program is not a trivial matter and must be dealt with on a proactive basis. Institutions with long-established on-ground programs unconsciously become inflexible in areas relating to faculty governance, workloads, administrative requirements, and financial practices. Online requires the re-definition of many of these traditional processes. A high priority and adequate resources need to be dedicated to meeting the needs of "Institutional Readiness."

4. Online education has unique characteristics that make it different in some aspects, than on-ground education. It is a critical error to assume that anyone who has been a successful teacher can take a successful on-ground program and just start teaching it online. While faculty who see value in the online approaches can learn online methodologies and become successful online facilitators, training is required to highlight these differences and provide tools to manage these differences. If faculty are unwilling to invest in developing online skills, they

should not be asked to participate in teaching online classes.

5. It is inevitable that comparisons will be made between online and on-ground. Focusing on the good of one over the weaknesses of the other will not be productive. Both processes are valid and can produce excellent results when properly administered in an appropriate setting. When online processes and tools are discussed, it should be recognized that most of these elements came from established on-ground concepts and most could be (or may currently be) used successfully in EITHER educational medium. The deciding factor in which of the processes to use is, or should be, based mostly on the accessibility of the education to the student. If there is an advantage in online, it is the **necessity** for carefully considering the elements of a program in detail to assure that the online processes used will support the delivery of the planned learning objectives. Online is unforgiving and demands that it be done thoughtfully from the onset.

6. Technology must be kept in the perspective of a tool - and not be allowed to take time away from the objective of an online program - to educate. Today, a number of new platforms with high levels of very seductive hi-tech features are being offered. While interesting to observe, and at first glance appealing to the marketplace, most are not essential to offering education online. These features ultimately become excessive cost factors, difficult hurdles for the non-technical student, excess time consumers for faculty, and general distracters from the educational objectives of a well-designed program. While we do not discourage innovation - in fact we support meaningful innovation in the most enthusiastic way - we caution you to keep the role of technology in

the proper perspective as you design your programs -
TECHNOLOGY IS ONLY A TOOL!

We sincerely hope that these comments will be helpful in
establishing a context in which to consider the contents of
the book.

About the authors

This book was written by the Socrates Distance Learning
Technology Group team, with home offices in Glendale,
Arizona. Team members are Gerry L. Bedore Jr. MBA, Dr.
Marlene R. Bedore, and Dr. Gerry L. Bedore.

The team owes special thanks to Mike Holtzman at THEN
Corporation of Westwood, California, who provided us the
opportunity to work with UCLA in the online programs;
Kathy McGuire of UNEX, who managed the development
and implementation of the Certificate of Completion in
Online Teaching; Paul Zagnoni of Academic Research and
Technologies; and Convene Corporation and Embanet, who
provided technical services and input. A special thank you
to Dr. Steve Williams, founder of the Baker College Online
Programs, who contributed immeasurably to the
advancement of online and to this book. Dr. Williams
continues to be a thought leader in the emerging paradigm.

1

Facilitators

Technology Students Curriculum

Balance

Overview

Distance learning

More and more students every day, across cities and around the world, pursue educational courses, either for academic credit or not, via their computers, with the help of distance learning programs. Distance learning is broadly defined as learning that occurs in an environment other than a physical classroom with other students and an instructor present. In distance learning models, a physical classroom is not necessary; a virtual classroom (VC) will suffice, and the students and facilitator can be scattered around the globe.

Distance learning online

Online is one specialized type of distance learning. In an online scenario, classes are conducted in a VC located "somewhere in a computer." Students can be located anywhere they can use a computer, a modem, and a telephone line. An instructor, or facilitator, can be anywhere else that meets the same physical requirements.

All are connected at appropriate times through normal telephone lines or across the Internet. Various technologies can be used to provide distance learning, and while several online models have been developed, this chapter focuses on an asynchronous or store-and-forward model. Other models will be discussed in later chapters.

> *Using a personal computer and modem, students enter the classroom almost anytime they choose.*

Learning institutions and corporations offer a variety of distance learning courses in the social and physical sciences, the humanities, foreign languages, writing, music, theater, and computer instruction, as well as a wide range of undergraduate and graduate studies degree program. An increasing number of different educational programs are available in completely online formats.

Using a personal computer and modem, students enter the classroom almost anytime they choose. It's open 24 hours a day, seven days a week. Online education is one of the great advents in education, and it is a cutting-edge movement. The learning process is similar to that in a traditional university; it is the environment that is different. Courses are taught by faculty members or instructors who are skilled in facilitation techniques. Classroom activities include lectures; questions are asked and answers are challenged. Assignments are given, student work is assessed, and feedback is provided, online, in the VC or privately. Students discuss topics by posting comments, questions, and observations, which become part of the ongoing text-supported seminar instruction. Extracurricular discussions and personal exchanges become a vital part of the online learning experience.

In many learning communities, as many as 95% of students have no online experience before enrolling in such a program. Students are interested in the flexibility and creditability of the courses as well as the technology. Most programs are designed to provide maximum flexibility to students who cannot participate in traditional programs. As they become involved with the technology, students appreciate the 24-hour access to the online campus. Students have many questions at the beginning of courses, and they log onto their VC three to five times a week. By the end of the

> *...it makes no sense for adults to be bound by time and place when it comes to learning essential new skills.*

first course, as students' attitudes improve and comfort levels increase, many log on three to five times a day.

The number of universities and corporations in the U.S. offering online educational programs increases daily. People are eager to learn and are excited about the ways new technology energizes the age-old quest for knowledge. In the article ("Earn a Masters, Virtually," Phillips, V., *Internet World*, 1996), distance learning is shown to be highly evolved and growing. Vicky Phillips cites universities and corporations that are using distance learning to expand their markets. Phillips states "Technology and a ready market are causing cyber graduate schools to take off" and contrasts traditional and distance learning:

> ...graduate schools. Ivy-espaliered towers of learning. Dark library walls graced with portraits of bespectacled academic deans. These picturesque concepts of the Ivy League are quietly being challenged by a

new vision of the university for the 21st century: the cyber league...While brick and ivy graduate schools will not disappear, their reach is being extended through the growth of electronic universities. Today, video conferencing allows faculties to be seen and heard across campus and across continents. Passionately silent classroom discussions on topics from network security to the poetry of T.S. Eliot take place via mailing lists. Managers from Bombay to London meet with geographically far-flung colleagues in e-conferencing halls to tackle the best ways to motivate their work groups. The pioneering faculty and students of the cyber league are fervently at work creating the first keyboard-accessible graduate schools for advanced learning...in society it makes no sense for adults to be bound by time and place when it comes to learning essential new skills...

What is online learning?

As mentioned previously, online learning is learning from where you are, as opposed to moving yourself to a physical classroom each time a class is to be held. If you have a personal computer, a modem, and a telephone line, you have the technical requirements for participating in classes that meet in cyberspace.

Ralph E. Goenory, in his keynote address to the Second International ALN Conference (Nov. 1996, New York City) states:

> To date, education, even higher education, which is the part of education we are

discussing today, has not been friendly to technology. Edison's electric light has been accepted, along with central heating, ball-point pens, and white boards. All these are firmly established in our classrooms, but until very recently the electronic revolution that has so significantly affected other industries, has mainly meant better-typed essays in academia.

Nevertheless, it is a fact that we are in possession today, not tomorrow, but today, of technologies that properly used, do enable learning to leap over the limitations that have always bound the professor and his or her class to be in the same place at the same time. The technical possibility exists to cut free of both the synchronies of time and of place that have characterized learning to date.[1]

The realization of this technical potential will strongly affect both the activities and the structure of the higher education industry as it has others. Today's cheap, fast, and convenient technology of computing, storing, and transmitting will only get cheaper, faster, and easier to use, but it is good enough today that we do not have to be content with visions of future education scenarios based on home video and broadband interaction. We do not even need to confine ourselves any longer to small scale experiments. We can and should do something significant in education and in training today.

---

[1] See the article, *Learning Outside the Classroom— The Time Is Now.*

In many cases, courses completed through online programs (for credit, certification, acquisition of skills, CEUs, etc.) are accredited just like similar course work completed on a campus. Regional accreditation committees (e.g., North Central Association) acknowledge and accept programs offered online as being equal educationally to those presented in a traditional format.

Programs accessed through a telephone line and a modem can cost more than those offered by traditional methods, but the conveniences are many, and the overall expense can be less than for traditional offerings. Sometimes connection charges and telephone-use fees are included in tuition, and sometimes they are not.

> *We can and should do something significant in education and in training today.*

For example, a student named Phil at Baker College in Flint, Michigan, is enrolled in several online courses in pursuit of a Master's degree. He attends classes from his home in Phoenix, Arizona, uses an AT&T direct access number to connect to the university's computers, and pays about $15.00 a month for long distance connection charges. Of course, Phil could connect through an Internet provider, but he thinks the direct dialing option best suits his needs.

Another hypothetical student's connection charges are included in the tuition at the New School for Social Research in New York. This student, a resident of Toronto, Ontario, dials into a Canadian network, which is linked to a large U.S. computer system, which connects to the school in New York.

Administration can be accomplished online. Many universities and corporations offer online registration, online bookstores, and online help desks. Online programs are designed to accommodate customers.

Online programs often take less time to complete than their on-campus counterparts. It is not unusual for a traditional 14-week course of study to be completed in five or six weeks using an online format.

> *Technology is vital, but it is only a set of tools.*

Developing an online program that affords this ease of use, this tremendous flexibility, and this creative learning experience demands adherence to a few fundamentals. These fundamentals will be discussed in the following section.

Elements of the online model

The online model consists of three key elements that surround the needs of the student, as illustrated by the diagram below. These are the facilitator, the curriculum, and the technology. These elements must be fully integrated and well balanced. The curriculum must be compatible with the facilitation process, and both must be compatible with the technology. Technology is vital, but it is only a set of tools.

The key elements, as shown in the following diagram, are discussed in detail in the following chapters.

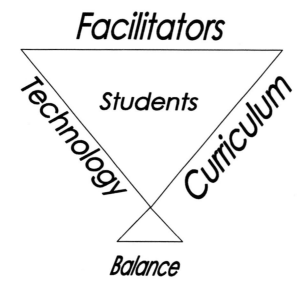

2

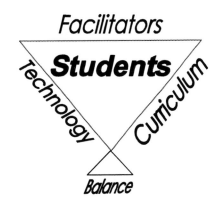

Facilitators
Students
Technology
Curriculum
Balance

The Student

Who is the online student? Why would someone pick an online college experience over the more traditional on-ground college? Is the online student looking for an easy way around the need for a college education? Is online education for everyone? Interesting questions—let's look at some of the answers.

Who is the online student?

The people who attend online learning programs vary. They include working adults, people living in remote locations, those who are physically challenged, and others.

- Most individuals using online learning programs are working adults who want to increase their capabilities and opportunities in the workplace. Setting aside several hours every week to further their education is the best they can do.

- Corporations place employees in online certification programs to enhance the employees' capabilities.

- People who cannot reach a learning facility because they live in rural areas frequently use online programs.

- Young people who want to further their education while pursuing careers find the flexible scheduling of online programs invaluable.

- Physically challenged people often find online learning a major convenience in extending their educational opportunities.

The online learning environment is ideal for continuing education programs. An expanding number of programs offer CEUs and certification opportunities as a means to expand and update one's current education.

Increasingly, professionals such as dentists, counselors, teachers, insurance agents, network engineers, and many others are finding online programs ideal for maintaining all or part of their professional accreditation. New programs are being developed for physicians, pharmacists, and other highly skilled professionals to help them conveniently access the new information they need to maintain a high level of performance in their chosen professions.

> *The online learning environment is ideal for continuing education programs.*

Students who graduated from college five to 10 years ago are finding themselves "obsolete" in their current workplace and need a refresher or even a new career opportunity. This can be done in parallel with their current work without taking time off or losing pay.

Programs are under way in major institutions throughout the United States that offer opportunities such as creative writing, English as a second language, flight ground schools, entrepreneur development, small business management, and more than 4,000 other special interest courses.

And the online concepts are relatively new, with most models being developed in just the past 10 years! Students from all walks of life, young and old, are finding interesting and convenient opportunities in the online world.

Why pick an online college?

The online process relies on a curriculum designed to stimulate dialogue among students and the facilitator. To achieve learning outcomes, the learning process includes the work, lives, and educational experiences of the students and the facilitator. The model is based on applications, and the knowledge learned today can be used in the workplace tomorrow. This environment is not based on lectures, memorization, and tests; it requires that faculty and students take an active part in the process, think critically, and apply concepts to real-time events.

Is online the easy way out?

Some still consider an online program as little more than a correspondence course and suggest that the merit of an online course is questionable in academic terms. This is simply untrue and will be rejected by most who try a course. Accreditation bodies are approving online programs for application to degree programs, and certification institutions are doing the same. The credibility of online is enhanced by the many premier educational institutions that are now offering for-credit courses and programs.

One of the reasons for the improving acceptance of online programs is the effort that is required for a student to successfully complete the requirements of a program. To receive accreditation from a regional accreditation group, it must be clearly demonstrated that the time requirements of an online course are equivalent to those by the on-ground equivalent classes. The agency must be convinced, using valid data, that the learning that takes place is equivalent or better than that obtained in the on-ground equivalent course. (This is discussed in more detail elsewhere in this book.) Research demonstrates that students studying in an online environment are measurably equivalent (and in many cases, superior) in learning to their on-ground counterparts.

> *Students participating in online classes are satisfied that they are receiving quality education with added flexibility relating to location and schedule.*

Most online programs are accelerated. The format in which an online subject is taught normally reduces the course time from the typical 14 weeks to five or six weeks. Most students take only one course at a time and normally spend ten to twelve hours a week on the course in study and group activities. The work is usually completed off-line, and the time spent online is only the few seconds a day necessary to transfer work to and from the host system. A normal online program requires that students sign on five days each week and contribute substantively to the activities. Students who are traveling can use portable equipment to do the day's lessons.

Most students surveyed indicate that they spend more time when participating in an online class than they do in on-ground classes. They say that it may take longer to complete the work; however, they are satisfied that they are receiving quality education with added flexibility relating to location and schedule. They also indicate that in many cases, their work and personal obligations would prohibit their participation in advancing their education if it weren't for the online option. They unanimously feel that they did not elect an easier method!

Is online for everyone?

Online is NOT for everyone, but it is suitable for most individuals. The state of most program technologies and developments probably would prohibit student programs at grade school and intermediate/middle school levels from online delivery. These areas are receiving attention; in the near future (one to three years), they will likely be served by an expanding number of online opportunities.

> *Ideal online programs are intuitive and require few computer skills.*

Some institutions are offering a limited number of programs to the average college student. There is no technical or social reason why this is not appropriate. The biggest deterrent is the resistance of traditional programs to offering for-credit courses in the relatively undisciplined online environment.

Some institutions are entering the online arena by offering tutorial services, library and research source access, administrative process access, and other non-credit support activities. This is changing; in three to five years, an abundance of courses will be available to the "educational shopper."

Currently, most successful programs focus on the adult learner. Even adult learners must be self-starters with sufficient discipline to maintain the pace of a typical program. If one procrastinates for a day or two, the fast-paced program may pass them by so that catching up is difficult or impossible.

A student need not be a computer guru. In fact, the ideal programs are very intuitive and require few computer-related skills. Newer software is self-installing and can be used with as little as one or two hours of orientation.

In summary, where there is a need and a desire for delivery of education away from a campus, online learning is adaptable. Students can use the self-evaluation instrument illustrated at the end of this chapter to determine if they will be comfortable learning online.

Student Self-Evaluation Instrument

Distance Learning! What is it?

What kinds of people are in distance learning programs? This 'SELF EVALUATION' is designed to help you decide if Distance Learning is right for you. The online learning process is not the same as a traditional learning program. This process requires that the curriculum, the manner in which the learning objectives are obtained, and the technology be matched.

Distance learning takes on many faces. The technologies emerging today are creating many variations in distance learning programs. This 'SELF EVALUATION' will focus on the asynchronous online model.

In order to help you make a decision about online learning, the following information is provided for your consideration:

- What is an asynchronous online learning model?
- What kinds of people are right for online learning programs?
- What programs are available online?
- How long do the courses last?
- What kind of computer skills are needed?
- What is the cost of an online education?
- What is an asynchronous online learning model?

The asynchronous learning process leans heavily on a curriculum that is designed to stimulate dialogue among the students and facilitator. In achieving the learning outcomes, the learning process utilizes the work, life, and educational experiences together with supplemental contemporary readings and various ancillaries to accelerate the learning curve. The model is heavily applications based and the knowledge learned today can be used in the workplace today. This environment is not based on lectures, memorization, and tests; it does require that the faculty and students take an active part in the process. Critical thinking and applying concepts to real time events is paramount.

What kinds of people are right for online learning programs?

The kinds of people who attend online learning programs vary. These are often busy working people who utilize the online process to enhance their capabilities and opportunities in the workplace. Many do not have the time to attend a traditional learning institution. Carving a couple of hours out of a few days a week to further their education is the best they can do. Corporations place employees in online educational and certification programs to enhance the employees' capabilities while allowing the employees to continue to produce for the company. People who do not have access to appropriate learning facilities can utilize online learning programs to meet their educational objectives. People who want to get their education while working can do both utilizing the online process. If you are the kind of person that wants to attend a traditional campus and go through a traditional program the online model may not be the best alternative for you.

What programs are available online?

A growing number of courses offered in a traditional format are being provided online. A student can now complete a degree from the first day as a freshman in college through a Ph.D. Many learning institutions and private companies offer certification programs online. The range of courses offered include but are not limited to:

Science	Medicine	Arts
Math	Technologies	Music
Business	Language	English

Most online academic programs are fully accredited.

How long do the courses last?

The format in which an online subject is taught normally "compresses" the course time from a traditional 14 weeks to an online format of six weeks. Most students take no more than 1 course at a time. An online student will normally spend 4 to 6 hours a week for each course. Most of the work is done off-line and the time spent online is only seconds a day. A typical online program requires the student sign on 5 of 7 days each week. If the student travels, a portable computer can be used to do the day's lesson.

What kind of computer skills are needed?

The computer and technology is only a tool utilized in this process. Most people entering an online program have very limited, if any computer experience. A short orientation course is offered in most online programs that assists the student in how to function in a Virtual Classroom. Attending a virtual classroom is easy and most people can do it effectively after a one-week orientation. Remember there are no buildings in an online program. The classroom is in cyberspace.

What is the cost of an online education?

The cost of an online program is generally about equal to the cost of a traditional program given all of the associated costs of attending a traditional program.

Am I a candidate for an online program?

The following is a brief questionnaire designed to help you discover if you are right for the online learning process. Respond to the questions; change your answers as much as you need until you're comfortable with your responses. Then compare your results to the notes in the analysis.

SELF-EVALUATION FOR POTENTIAL ONLINE <u>STUDENTS</u>

Here are some basic questions to ask yourself in deciding if the online program is right for you:

		YES	NO
1.	Do you have (or are you willing to obtain) access to a computer and phone line at home?	☐	☐
2.	Do you feel that high quality learning can take place without going to a traditional educational facility?	☐	☐
3.	Do you like the idea of sharing your work, life, and educational experiences as part of the learning process?	☐	☐
4.	Can you make 4 to 6 hours a week (anytime during the day or night) available to participate in the learning process?	☐	☐
5.	Are you a self- motivated and self- disciplined person?	☐	☐
6.	Are you comfortable in communicating in writing?	☐	☐
7.	Do you see value in being able to think an idea through before having to give a response?	☐	☐
8.	Do you subscribe to the value of introducing critical thinking into the learning process?	☐	☐
9.	Do you see the possibility of increased learning taking place when work/ life/ knowledge experiences are shared with peers?	☐	☐
10.	Do you accept the value of facilitated learning as an advantage over the more traditional lecture based learning processes?	☐	☐

<u>ANALYSIS OF YOUR RESPONSES</u>:

Look carefully at your responses. To be a good candidate for an online program, you should have answered YES to questions 1, 4, and 6.

In addition, you should have answered YES to 5 of the remaining 7 questions. If you did not meet this criteria, you should talk to an enrollment counselor prior to registering for an online class.

SOCRATES©
Distance Learning Technologies Group
6737 W Union Hills Drive
Glendale, Arizona 85308

3

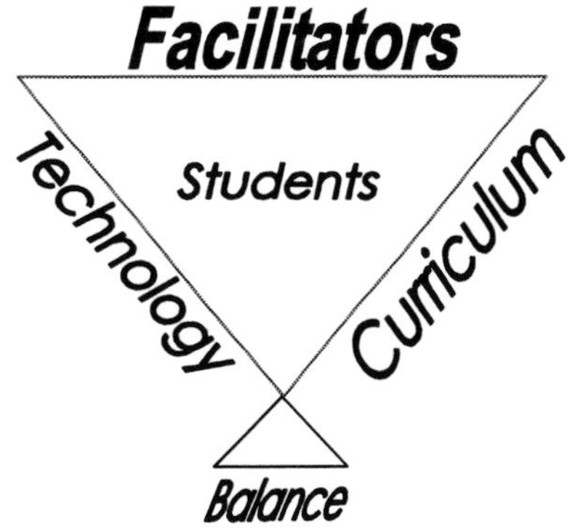

Facilitators

Technology

Students

Curriculum

Balance

The Facilitator

Introduction

When discussing this element of the model, the terms "instructor," "facilitator," and "faculty member" are all used. The designation refers to the level of education being offered. For example, in corporate educational programs, instructors are often corporate employees who have expertise in a particular field but lack formal academic credentials. On the other hand, in an MBA program, the faculty member is likely to hold a doctoral degree. Regardless of specific credentials, all online instructors function as facilitators.

Online instructors usually are well trained, both in their subject matter and in how the online learning process works. The ability to manage curricula, tools, and technologies to achieve learning goals requires training and practice. Instructors who have been highly successful in traditional classrooms sometimes question the need for specialized training in teaching online. It is important that all parties involved in the online paradigm recognize that it is substantially different than on-ground alternatives.

Online models are predicated on a facilitative model, in contrast to traditional lecture-based models. This, together with the differences in the mechanical process, makes successful online teaching a process that requires acceptance, understanding of the differences between models, and experience.

> *All parties in the online paradigm must realize that it differs substantially from traditional teaching.*

Training is a key ingredient. To develop a better understanding of the skills required to operate an online program, we are going to look at one model of a facilitator training program.

Facilitator selection

As will be noted as you read this book, the online environment is unique in many areas. These unique aspects make the selection of those teaching—or facilitating—courses very critical to the success of the programs. More specifically, teaching online is not for everyone—it is for many, but not for all.

The concern for who will be successful as an online instructor will come to light early in the discussions of programs being implemented in existing institutions. Will the teacher we have now be the core of our online teaching staff? Unfortunately, experience indicates that the answer to this is usually no! This is the beginning of a series of related challenges including the selection of successful facilitators.

The "Faculty Self-Evaluation Instrument" at the end of this chapter can be used in several ways to assist in the selection process. First, it is frequently supplied to inquiring instructors to be used as a self-selection tool. The document is designed to provide key requirements for being a successful online facilitator. A series of questions follows that will assist the inquirer in getting in touch with these requirements in a practical way. The candidate decides if he or she fits and then proceeds in the process only if he or she is satisfied that success is probable.

Second, this document can be used as an interview tool to assist in qualifying applicants for online teaching assignments. The person interviewing candidates may want to customize the materials to provide ways to assure that the candidate understands the expectations and then evaluate the degree to which the candidate qualifies for the various elements.

The selection process needs to be comprehensive and critical. The institution will spend money on training, and will grant a great degree of academic freedom to this facilitator in determining how the subject will be taught. In general, the facilitator will be the key to the success of the class, the model that students will use to evaluate whether they want to continue in the program, and the benchmark for students to communicate to their peers regarding the quality of the online program.

Successful on-ground instruction is not necessarily an indicator of the ability of one to perform online. This is indicated in the materials in the evaluation form and should be considered with great care as one considers a current on-ground instructor for possible online work. The next version of this book will dedicate a chapter to facilitator selection. In the meantime, the materials provided here should serve as a guide. You may want to seek consultant support for your early selection and evaluation efforts.

The three-week+ facilitator training model

This model includes the following elements:

- Candidates for facilitator training are sought according to the needs of the program. Candidates are pre-qualified, based on their credentials and interests (self-selection is often used as a sorting tool).

- Selected candidates enter a three-week online training program designed to introduce them to online processes and tools and to make them comfortable with the technology.

- After successfully completing the three-week program, trainees enter the mentorship phase, which is like a finishing school for facilitators. Under the guidance of an accomplished online program mentor, trainees develop and prepare course materials, including a syllabus, and experience their first online teaching.

- After successfully completing the mentorship phase, trainees are classified in terms of their readiness for online teaching assignments.

This is only a summary of the training model; details are provided in Chapter 4.

Instructor training

The Socrates training portfolio offers several approaches to instructor training. The needs of each institution vary; the approach selected depends on several factors, including:

- computer literacy levels of individuals being trained

- application software being used by the institution (proprietary, Convene, commercial, etc.)

- flexibility of student instructors in terms of time dedicated to training

- responsibilities of instructors in the total curriculum/teaching process

- online experience levels of student instructors and the institution

- the culture of the sponsoring institution

- objectives of the program (degree, certificate, general interest, etc.)

- influence of Total Quality Management (TQM) or other quality concepts on the processes used by the institution

Targeted training level

Some training issues are judged by seasoned on-ground instructors to be relatively low level, but the intent of this training is to provide support at the level of the lowest common denominator in the group being trained. Those who have more skills tend to skim over elementary materials during training.

Training simulates the VC

It is beneficial to conduct training of this type in an online mode, using much the same dialogue and tools that today's student instructors will use tomorrow with their students in a VC. This aspect gives student instructors a feel for and some experience in implementing generic online learning models.

The length of training programs

Many programs are customized to meet the needs of the people involved. Some guidelines follow:

- If the student instructor is already a fully qualified online instructor, institutional orientation alone is usually sufficient. This can be accomplished in five sessions, usually conducted in one week.

  Note: The duration of a session varies from a few minutes to an hour, depending on the complexity of the task and the skill of the student. Sessions normally are conducted off-line, at the convenience of the student, any time within a 24-hour period. After completing a task, the student signs online, and the duration of the link to the system is only a few seconds.

- If the student instructor must change from one application platform to another (e.g., from a proprietary system to Convene), five sessions should suffice and usually can be concurrent within the institutional orientation.

- The training of a person who is unfamiliar with online processes must be divided into at least two major phases. The first phase emphasizes the mechanical procedures used in online environments. This phase usually can be taught in three weeks (15 sessions), but does not fully prepare the student instructor for the VC experience, only for the technology.

To supplement training received in the first phase and to ensure that instructors and their students in the future enjoy successful VC experiences, the second phase consists of a mentorship. This phase focuses on interactive classroom processes, how to prepare a syllabus that supports the supplied curriculum, and how to use online VC tools.

Mentorship, in which experienced instructors share materials and knowledge with student instructors, is a preferred method of teaching. It involves qualified instructors who monitor student instructors' practice teaching activities in the VC. Mentors communicate with those students outside the VC. Usually after one course of mentorship, student instructors' progress is assessed, and their needs for further development are defined and provided for.

- ◆ Student instructors who must be taught to develop or convert curricula from on-ground to online require additional skills on the part of the trainer. Normally, facilitators learn these skills by repeating the facilitation process in VC situations and, possibly, through supplemental training by the institution requesting the support. Someone with proven special skills in developing online course curricula can lead instructors through the process, ensuring that every outcome is consistent with the requirements of the institution.

This is only a partial list of the options available for pure online and hybrid programs. This list grows as new technologies become available and additional variations are developed. For example, Socrates is piloting eyeball cameras as tools, in conjunction with the Internet as a carrier, to perform selective one-on-one, group, and special presentations, with video as a means of projecting materials.

The successful instructor must develop skill with these tools. Those who are experienced in facilitative teaching will catch on quickly. Their only significant hurdle is becoming familiar with the medium. Those who are not already facilitators must develop these skills, adapt to the medium, and translate the tools to this medium.

> *The most effective way to develop online facilitators is through facilitator training followed by mentorship with an online instructor.*

This can be accomplished in various ways. The most effective way is through facilitator training, then by a

mentorship with an accomplished online instructor. The ideal model for this mentorship is for the student instructor to complete the training, observe a class taught by an accomplished instructor (preferably but not necessarily in the same discipline), and then facilitate a class with the guidance of the mentor.

The length of the mentorship varies from a couple of seminars to one or two full classes, and the student instructor's readiness is judged on observed performance under actual teaching conditions. Ideally, mentorships last a long time, during which the mentor and the new instructor exchange materials, ideas, and concerns. Mentors should be carefully selected, well compensated for what they do, and viewed as valuable members of the quality control team. The degree to which this process is applied can vary, depending on the facilitative experience of the student instructor.

Mentorships often are slighted because they add cost, take time, and may seem somewhat intrusive. This apparent downside must be weighed against the risks of not thoroughly preparing facilitators for actual conditions. These risks include damaged classes, poor student experiences, loss of students due to the extension of bad perceptions to other classes, loss of instructors due to their poor and frustrating experiences, and a negative impact on the word-of-mouth benefits that can be gained from satisfactory student-instructor experiences.

The following diagram profiles a typical instructor training program

Socrates DLTG
Instructor Training Profile

RECRUITMENT & SELECTION	ONLINE TRAINING	MENTORSHIP	ASSIGNMENTS	ONGOING MONITORING

RECRUITMENT & SELECTION

<u>See Recruitment & Selection</u>

ONLINE TRAINING

<u>Trainer</u>

Provides structured training

Evaluates participation & progress

Recommends pass/fail training

Is consultant to all instructors

<u>"Student" instructor</u>

Three week duration

5 of 7 participation

Mandatory for all new online instructors

Heavy focus on process and technology skills

MENTORSHIP

<u>Mentor</u>

Qualified mentor must have taught at least three class online

Does not have to be content specific

Provides guidance for syllabus preparation

Monitors first class

Evaluates/corrects

Peer evaluator role after 1st class

Reviews student end-of-course surveys /recommends any further development needs

<u>"Student" instructor</u>

Complete online training

Prepare for first class with guidance from mentor

Teaches class with mentor observing

Approved for further assignments or additional training

ASSIGNMENTS

<u>Mentor</u>

Available for questions & support

<u>"Student" instructor</u>

Placed in assignment pool

Preferred status for first "untethered" assignment

Received 10% increase after completing 3 classes

5% more after 10 classes

ONGOING MONITORING

<u>See Quality Programs</u>

Faculty Self-Evaluation Instrument

Online Learning Model

The online learning process is not the same as a traditional learning program. It cannot be taught the same way a traditional program would be. To do this, the online learning process leans heavily on curriculum that is designed to stimulate dialogue between the students and the facilitator. Facilitators/instructors teaching in the online model oversee the Virtual Classroom and take the necessary actions to ensure the dialogue and student interaction is consistent with defined learning outcomes. In achieving the learning outcomes the learning processes utilizes the work, life, and educational experiences of the students and facilitator to enhance the learning curve.

The online model is heavily applications based. The things learned today can be used in the workplace tomorrow. The use of 'Clinical Faculty' is preferred in the online paradigm. It is critical that the facilitator/instructor be able to relate the curriculum to the work place and the workplace to the curriculum. The online environment is not based on lectures, memorization, and tests. It is based on achieving the learning outcomes by synthesizing theory and real world experience. The process requires that the facilitator/instructor and students take an active part. The facilitator/instructor cannot give a lecture along with some reading and go home for the day. Monitoring the VC and being a part of the learning experience is required. Critical thinking and applying concepts to real time events is paramount in the process.

Who Attends Online Programs?

The kinds of people who attend online learning programs vary. There are busy working people who utilize the online process to enhance their capabilities and opportunities in the workplace. These people do not have the time to attend a traditional learning institution. Carving a couple of hours out of a few days a week to further their education is the best they can do. This requires the instructor/facilitator be flexible and concerned with the students' success.

Corporations place employees in online educational and certification programs to enhance the employees capabilities while allowing the employees to continue to produce for the company. Many people who do not have access to a year round learning facility utilize online programs to compensate for living in remote locations or a lack of appropriate facilities in their areas. People, who want to get their education while working, can do both utilizing the online process.

Many educational courses offered in a traditional format are offered online. Students can now do a complete degree online. From the first day as a freshman to a Ph.D. More and more learning institutions and private companies are offering certification programs. The range of courses offered include but are not limited to:

Science	Medicine	Arts
Math	Technologies	Music
Business	Language	Many others

Many online learning education programs have full recognition by accrediting agencies. Generally, online programs are accelerated. The format in which an online subject is taught normally reduces the course time from a traditional 14 weeks to an online format of 6 weeks. Students take no more than one course at a time. An online student will normally spend 4 to 6 hours a week for each course. Most of the work is done off-line and the time spent online is only seconds a day. A normal online program requires the student sign on 5 of 7 days each week. If the student is traveling they can utilize a portable computer to do the days lesson, "from where they are". The instructor/facilitator normally views the VC daily to ensure things are moving as they should. Participating in the class 5 of 7 days a week is essential. This can be done from anywhere you have a computer and phone line. The online learning process allows tremendous flexibility in lifestyle.

The Role of the Computer & Technologies

The computer and technology are only tools in the online process. Most people entering an online program have very limited, if any computer experience at all. A short orientation course is offered in most online programs to assist the student in how to function in a Virtual Classroom. Facilitators/instructors generally attend a 3- to 6-week training program to familiarize them with the software and the techniques utilized in teaching online. Attending a virtual classroom is easy and most people can do it effectively after a one-week orientation. Remember there are no buildings in an online program. The classroom is in cyberspace.

What Are the Expectations for an Online Facilitator?

In order to develop and maintain an online program that is effective, smooth, and that will achieve the learning outcomes as required, the facilitator will play a vital role. While many highly seasoned instructors within the traditional realm will easily adapt to the online model, many will not. Seeing the need for online instructor training is often underestimated . The facilitator in the online environment must possess a unique set of tools to perform effectively. Some of the basic elements of what kind of person is right for facilitating an online course and what capabilities they should posses are:

1. The facilitator should be able to present the curriculum in a manner that allows the student to easily translate theories into applications.

2. The facilitator should be able to create a learning environment that utilizes life, work, and educational experiences as key elements in the learning process.

3. Facilitators in the online arena are generally considered to be 'Clinical'. That is, they have a broad base of experiences and a solid business related background.

4. The facilitator should do little or no lecturing. Lecturing is the least productive method of teaching.

5. The facilitator should not subject students to tests requiring memorization. Case analysis would be more appropriate.

6. The facilitator should be able to accept the value of facilitated learning over the traditional learning model.

7. The facilitator should feel comfortable communicating in writing.

8. The personality of the facilitator should demonstrate the characteristics of openness, concern, flexibility, and sincerity.

9. The facilitator should be online everyday (at minimum 5 of 7 days).

10. The facilitator should be able to subscribe to the value of introducing critical thinking into the learning process.

11. The facilitator should reasonably accommodate the students needs and desires.

12. The facilitator should be concerned about the students' success.

13. The facilitator should have the appropriate credentials to teach the subject matter.

14. The facilitator should be able to give the students the proper tools to transcribe theory into practice.

15. The facilitator should be able to give every student the opportunity to improve until the learning experience come to an end.

16. The facilitator should be experienced and well trained in online learning experience.

17. The facilitator should solicit feedback from the students and listen through to entire process.

18. The facilitator should be able to treat students politely and with respect.

These are not all of the expectations. The idea is to give the reader a general overview as to what behaviors and practices create successful online facilitators.

SELF-EVALUATION FOR POTENTIAL ONLINE FACULTY

Here are some basic questions to ask yourself in deciding if the online program is right for you:

		YES	NO
1.	Do you have (or are you willing to obtain) access to a computer and phone line at home?	☐	☐
2.	Do you feel that high quality learning can take place without going to a traditional educational facility?	☐	☐
3.	Do you like the idea of sharing your work, life, and educational experiences as part of the learning process?	☐	☐
4.	Can you make 4 to 6 hours a week (anytime during the day or night) available to participate in the teaching process?	☐	☐
5.	Are you a self- motivated and self- disciplined person?	☐	☐
6.	Are you comfortable communicating in writing?	☐	☐
7.	Do you see value in being able think about an idea before having to give a response?	☐	☐
8.	Do you subscribe to the value of introducing critical thinking in the learning process?	☐	☐
9.	Do you see the possibility of increased learning taking place when work/ life/ knowledge experiences are shared with peers?	☐	☐
10.	Do you accept the value of facilitated learning as an advantage over the more traditional lecture based learning processes?	☐	☐
11.	Do you have the appropriate credentials to teach the subject matter?	☐	☐
12.	Are you willing to participate (on your own time) in an extensive training and mentorship program in preparation for teaching assignments?	☐	☐

ANALYSIS OF YOUR RESPONSES:

Look carefully at your responses. Most successful online instructors answer YES to Questions 1, 4, 6, 11, and 12 as well as YES to five of the seven remaining questions.

If your answers did not fall as indicated above, your interests are probably not aligned with the requirements of this teaching medium. Nevertheless, if you feel you want to explore possibilities in this area, please feel free to contact....

SOCRATES©

Distance Learning Technologies Group
6737 W Union Hills Drive
Glendale, Arizona 85308

4

Facilitators

Technology

Students

Curriculum

Balance

Faculty Training

Introduction

Research and experience indicates that there is no single preferred way to accomplish the training needs of online instructors. The tendency is to establish rigorous and highly structured training programs in a "one size fits all" approach. This is probably because it has always been done that way. When such models are used in the online paradigm, there seems to be a conflict between the "environment" of online programs and the structured nature of the training. The following question is often asked: Why is it necessary for rigid training processes when the virtual classroom model touts its free-form approach to learning?

In the ideal situation, requiring a course similar to the UCLA Extension program "The Certificate of Completion in Online Teaching" would assure that faculty entering the online program as instructors would provide a very high level of expected success for candidates. Such a program requires six to nine months to complete and would be difficult to impose as a mandatory requirement. Many adaptations of the materials presented in this program have been piloted with varying results depending on the background of the candidates and the requirements of the institution sponsoring the training.

This chapter presents two approaches to faculty training – the structured training model and the open model. The structured model has evolved over the past five years and has proven to be satisfactory in a wide range of situations. However, this model was initially developed when basic computer literacy could not be assumed for each person seeking to teach in the online model. Also, there were no experienced online instructors to bring their metaphors to the training process for sharing. This is changing – 90% of the instructors that come into the online environment are computer literate and in most cases – web proficient. In about 40% of the cases, the individuals have some exposure to online; this number is increasing. This makes reconsideration

> *Requiring a course similar to the UCLA Extension program "The Certificate of Completion in Online Teaching" assures that faculty provide a high level of success for candidates.*

of the training paradigm appropriate. The open model described below is one approach to providing for training in many emerging situations.

The facilitator life-cycle

The model below illustrates the steps involved in the recruiting/training/ongoing monitoring processes that take place in the life cycle of a faculty person. These steps must be met in some manner by the processes used in training and maintaining the faculty quality levels.

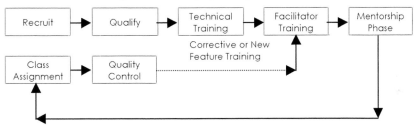

The requirements of this life cycle can be met in a number of ways. This chapter will look at two models for achieving this requirement—**the structured model** and **the open model**.

Structured models

The three-week online model has proven to be adequate in getting facilitators to the VC with enough confidence and ability to begin facilitating online. This model is designed to have a mentorship program supporting the process. This model is ideal for technical programs and programs being offered in institutions where online programs exist and a base level of knowledge exists concerning the paradigm.

A six-week model exists for those institutions and organizations that are particularly sensitive to the facilitation process. This model is also designed to be supported by a mentorship program. Organizations and institutions providing technical programs, operating in models other than the interactive and bounded interactive models, and having some experience with the online learning processes generally will not need to use the six-week model.

> *The structured model has been proven in a wide range of situations, but was developed before computer literacy could be assumed and before there were experienced online instructors.*

Open models

As noted in the introductory materials, we are increasingly dealing with more proficient faculty candidates and shorter timelines. The training needs of these people vary, but generally, they do not need to "start from ground zero." In many cases, asking the potential faculty to complete the full content of a structured program generates resistance and even resentment. Yet, the online paradigm is sufficiently different from on-ground programs that some form of orientation and facilitator training is essential.

The following diagram details how the open model fits into the general model above. This model replaces the Facilitator Training block in the general model.

The Open Model

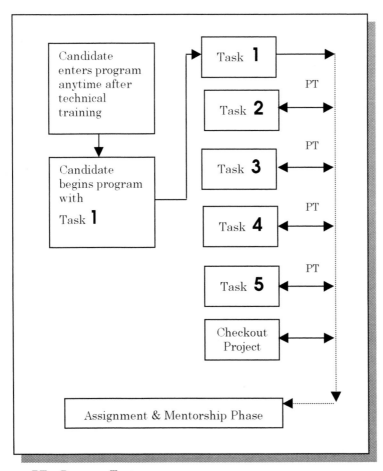

PT – Progress Test

The open model provides for the open entry/open exit of candidates to the facilitator training for those that have been recruited, qualified (academic credentials), and on the technology being utilized for the classes. The average candidate entering this training should be able to complete the elements in three to four weeks—even less if there is a concentrated effort on the part of the candidate. Candidates can proceed at their own pace through the five steps.

The five steps are provided in appropriate areas of the program being used and are available to the participants at any time during the process. Each segment has individual learning outcomes and simulations for the participant to use in measuring progress. In parallel with this independent effort, the student has access to the virtual classroom (VC) and the class facilitator. The training elements are designed to generate some dialogue in the

> *The open model provides for open entry/open exit of qualified candidates who have been trained on the technology.*

VC that will facilitate the involvement of students working at various levels in the overall training program. This will result in the sharing of knowledge and experiences between the participants. The following are examples of what the learning objectives of a facilitator training program include:

1. Familiarize the potential facilitator with different learning models used in asynchronous online learning programs.

2. Provide the potential with an overview of the facilitator's role within the varying models.

3. Provide an overview of the expectations of the facilitator, the student, the curriculum, and the technology. Examples are:

- ◆ commitment levels
- ◆ attitudes
- ◆ customer service expectations
- ◆ balances
- ◆ utility grade services
- ◆ others

4. Provide an overview of the mannerisms used in facilitating a successful virtual classroom.

5. Set up a virtual classroom (or branch meetings/work groups) within a given technology platform.

6. Provide an interactive experience in setting up a virtual classroom, posting a syllabus and other materials to the VC, and responding to comments coming into the VC.

7. Technology questions are answered.

Upon successful completion of the facilitator training, a mentor is assigned to support the new facilitator until such time as the facilitator is familiar and comfortable with the online environment. Continued online support to the facilitator is provided for an extended period of time.

> *The key to the overall process is the mentorship phase.*

The facilitator will be monitoring the VC and providing direction as appropriate to the participants. The facilitator's comments will be shared by all levels of participants, which will support the broadening of the exposure of all. The facilitator will also be available for private counseling and instruction and will be proactive in dealing with apparent problems or deficiencies in student progress.

The final step in the process is completion of the checkout project by the student. This project is designed to cause the candidate to demonstrate proficiency in the key facilitator tasks being taught in the program. Satisfactory completion of this event will constitute "graduation" and the candidate is ready for assignment to a mentor and to a class.

A key to the overall process is the mentorship phase. This is of particular importance to those with limited or no experience in a virtual classroom environment. No matter how much training one receives, the training is not complete until classroom experience is available. The mentorship activities assist the new instructor in successfully adjusting to the virtual classroom. This part of the process also reduces the risk for the institution when new facilitators enter a classroom. Potential problems can be spotted by the seasoned mentor and corrective actions taken before they become significant issues for the instructor and the institution.

Facilitator training will be provided in a flexible and comfortable online environment. The materials are posted to the virtual classroom area, and the course is self-paced with a defined period of time.

Faculty training models

The following table describes four primary models for new faculty (facilitator) training. The models are more detailed descriptions of the structured and open models previously discussed. Each model is designed to provide a level of knowledge consistent with the online teaching requirements of various institutions and to teach in one of the four functional models described in the following table.

These models are presented in an effort to provide understanding of what is recommended for instructors in various situations. It is appropriate to combine factors from multiple models into a unique custom model (if that is required at your institution). Such programs are normally done under some elapsed-time contract that focuses on even more precise institutional requirements.

The models and information described in this chapter are patterned from programs operated by a contract service providing these to corporations and institutions involved in online learning programs. Most of the concepts discussed can be developed and packaged by internal groups or consultant support to be offered internally or in other environments.

FACULTY/FACILITATOR TRAINING MODELS

TYPE	MODEL DESCRIPTION	CLASSROOM FORMAT	NOTES
1	Three-week structured model with 6/18 mentorship program	Multi-organizational classroom	Scheduled start dates
2	Open entry proficiency-based model (six-week limit)	Multi-organizational classroom	Mentorship priced separately
3	Three-week structured model with 6/18 mentorship program	Dedicated classroom	Scheduled start dates
4	Annual contract program with open or dedicated classroom and/or mentorships	Quotation as custom program	Scheduled start dates

All new faculty entering one of the optional programs is expected to have satisfactorily completed the initial technical training with the vendor supplying the online software before starting any of the options. It is not practical to pick up this training in parallel with the facilitator training.

Programs are available for any of the normal technologies used for online instruction, including Embanet, Convene, and Domino (an educational front-end for Lotus Notes).

Three-week structured model

The three-week structured model is designed to provide knowledge in the use of the technology to a level consistent with the average instructor. It is applicable to all models described in the summaries given later in this chapter, but is the minimum necessary for the interactive and bounded interactive models. This is because these models depend on a high level of facilitator skills for the classes to meet their objectives. As we move to the higher student count models, facilitator skills become less significant as independent study activities increase.

> *The 6/18 mentorship program picks up where facilitator training leaves off to help the new instructor transition to the classroom.*

The "6/18" mentorship program is part of this model and is designed to pick up where the facilitator training leaves off to assist the new facilitator in the transition to the actual classroom situation. This is a proven method for minimizing the difficulties of transitioning and improving the first class after training.

The multi-organization classroom is a classroom that may have students from several different companies and organizations participating in a common learning environment. This has proven to be an excellent method for improving the synergy that takes place in a shared learning environment. Since the materials covered are generally not of a proprietary nature, participants from different companies are welcomed for their contributions.

Structured classes have defined start dates, and the courses last three weeks. This is reflective of the structured lessons, assignments, and workshops that take place in this format.

The open-entry proficiency-based model

This model is similar in material coverage to the structured model described above. The significant difference is the self-study/self-pacing characteristics of this model. The course is designed to be completed in three weeks, but a student may choose to take up to six weeks to complete the work. The work is packaged in "modules" that are completed in a sequence. One module is completed and a "test" demonstrates proficiency in that module. The student is then free to progress to another model. A student may study several modules simultaneously, but will complete the proficiency demonstrations in sequence.

This program encourages sharing in a common virtual meeting place; however, this is limited by where a given student progresses within the program. The degree of completion will vary with most students in this configuration. In many ways, this process is self-study with consulting support from the facilitator, and final proficiency tests determine when the facilitator is ready to proceed to the classroom.

A student can enroll in the program today and begin classes the same day. There is no grouping of students for starting. Students can finish at any time their modules are completed but they must complete a program in six weeks or start again. This is to minimize administrative burdens on the part of the instructor/facilitators and to assure continuity of training.

This model is applicable to all program models but works best when entering facilitators are somewhat experienced in online instruction and are looking for specific assistance in an unfamiliar technology. This model is also adaptable to the higher-student count configurations described in the program models chart. In these models, the level of facilitator skills is reduced due to the increased emphasis on individual work.

The "6/18" mentorship program is optional in this configuration but is recommended where the new facilitator has limited experience in online programs.

Three-week structured model with dedicated classroom

The third alternative presented in the chart is the same as option one except for the dedicated classroom option. This

> *A student can enroll in the program and begin classes the same day.*

program is offered to institutions who feel that sharing with other organizations may compromise their security or objectives. This model is also applicable if there are custom features or materials to be included in the program—in other words, customized programs.

Annual contract programs

The programs suggested as Type 4 are intended to meet the needs of organizations who have special requirements, large training needs, or other special circumstances that require individualized support. The program designs will usually be constructed from parts of the options noted above. Pricing is quoted on a custom basis.

The "6/18" mentorship program

The "6/18" mentorship program is designed to pick up where the group training concludes and helps transition the new instructor into the actual virtual classroom experience. A trained and skilled mentor is assigned to each new instructor to follow this individual for a six-week class period. The mentor will be logged into the virtual classroom and monitor the interaction and content. The mentor will communicate privately with the new instructor as the class progresses to assure the instructor has opportunities to deal with real-time problems that may arise. The mentor will also work with the new instructor as they finalize the preparation of the course syllabus to ensure that the syllabus is workable. The "6/18" designation says that the mentor will work for six weeks, but this six weeks must occur within 18 weeks from the beginning of the new instructor training. This means that the new instructor will have to be assigned a class within 15 weeks of the conclusion of training or the training may be considered invalid—it is essential that the facilitator apply the skills from the training as soon as is reasonable after completion of training. The mentorship program is designed to support this requirement.

In summary

The success of most educational programs are a combination of well-developed concepts in multiple areas. This chapter focuses on the training of faculty that function in the online environment. Multiple models are required to meet the varying needs of organizations working with online programs.

It is important to carefully consider how the faculty are trained for online programs. The processes are very different than those for on-ground classes, and experience indicates that there must be paradigm transitions for those involved. Some institutions feel that faculty that are currently successful in on-ground classrooms can directly move to online programs; this, however, is only possible in very few cases.

The faculty need to put pressure on the system, and the tendency is to short-cut known successful approaches. This chapter provides a number of proven processes that will yield quality faculty and programs in a minimum of time and with the flexibility that goes with online education in general.

5

Facilitators

Technology

Students

Curriculum

Balance

The Curriculum

Educational curricula can be said to exist on a continuum, ranging from independent study at one end to the Socratic method at the other. The independent end of the continuum suggests that the student be required to obtain the knowledge on an independent basis. The Socratic end of the continuum argues that a group combines knowledge, experiences, and thought processes to derive answers. Between the extremes exists a mixture, with a facilitator playing a role to various degrees.

The learning continuum also can be viewed in terms of the synergy created at each point along the continuum. Synergy plays a vital role in online learning. The interactive online model exists slightly to the Socratic side of the middle of the continuum. Synergy levels along the continuum span from the highest point at the Socratic end to the lowest point at the independent study end, and may apply to other program models.

A learning continuum

The diagram below represents the learning continuum used by the authors to assist in visualizing the relationship between several models representing Facilitator-student involvement and synergy potentials. The model suggests that where the responsibility for learning is placed directly on the student, relatively low synergy expectations will be realized. The dialogue in such learning experiences is generally limited to a low level of prescribed written work that is reviewed by a faculty person and an equally minimal level of verbal communications between the faculty person, the student, and other students taking similar studies. The model also suggests that where a substantial discussion effort is encouraged between the faculty and student to student, a relatively high level of synergy can be accepted.

The curriculum design and the tools selected to achieve the planned learning must work together. This will assure that we generate sufficient discussion and interactions between the human elements of the process to contribute to the achievement of the desired learning outcomes. The way various exercises and assignments are combined will set the levels of dialogue that can take place in a workshop. The addition of other tools such as group activities and independent assignments will further impact the level of activities that will take place in the VC. As we will see when we review the various learning models later in this book, our knowledge of how to "regulate" or otherwise define the curriculum content will be imperative to successfully balancing the course factors.

The Learning Continuum

The typical online model
operates here

General Model Content					
Socratic	Facilitator -Student	Full Work Group	Small Work Group	Instructor -Student	Independent Study

High Synergy → Low Synergy

The Socratic method

This learning model assumes that all knowledge can be achieved through dialogue between students, with the guidance of a facilitator. All knowledge is said to exist in the experiences and thought processes of the participants. The range of the discussion is broad. Synergy is the highest of any point on the continuum.

The facilitator/student model

In this model, the facilitator guides the learning process, using various tools. The tools can be questions to stimulate critical thinking about the subject, text materials, the introduction of theories, or focused dialogue. The facilitator plays a heavy role in the process. The range of discussion is limited. Life experiences, work experiences, and accumulated knowledge are significant elements of this learning process. Synergy is higher than in the full workgroup model.

The full workgroup model

Participants work on projects as a group and discuss the outcomes. The facilitator guides the process by establishing formats and providing directional input to the group's processes. Text and other tools are used to achieve the learning objectives. It can be instructor-led, as opposed to facilitator-led. Synergy is higher than in the small workgroup model.

The small workgroup model

Participants are divided into small groups to work on projects. Each group's outcome is introduced to the class, where knowledge is shared. It is instructor-based and heavily guided. Synergy is moderate.

Instructor/student model

The instructor heavily guides the class. Students are assigned text readings, lectures are given, and tests are taken as the primary learning measure. Synergy is higher than in the independent study model.

Independent study model

Materials are given to the student with the learning objectives defined. Students must learn the material on their own. No instructor or facilitator is present. Synergy is the lowest of any point on the continuum.

Curriculum development

The curriculum for an online learning program is either newly generated or converted from an existing program, and then adapted using available tools and technology to achieve the learning objectives. When generating or converting a curriculum, consider the following questions:

- Will the curriculum be generated or modified from an existing curriculum?

- Who will develop the curriculum?

- How much technology will be included in the curriculum? Simulations? Grammar checkers? Statistical packages?

Assuming that the institution offers programs in the online format that are identical to the on-ground classes, existing curricula can act as a baseline. Often, curricula can be modified to fit the online format and the duration of the classes. Many exercises require modification or replacement. Individual and group activities require consideration, and technological issues, particularly in quantitative courses, require action. When new or modified programs are offered, new curricula must be developed. Curriculum development skills for online offerings are unique and must be part of the timing and provisioning considerations.

The following questions were asked by an organization regarding a curriculum for an online program.

Q. What additional training, if any, is required to enable someone to convert a class curriculum from a physical classroom to a virtual classroom?

A. Supplemental training options vary according to the backgrounds and experience of the people you want to convert the curricula. Variations are possible, but we have found that the following suggestions can be beneficial:

1. Someone who knows the online paradigm should provide a set of standards for curricula to serve as a guide. Because of variations in the presentation of subject areas, the standards must be flexible.

2. Offer an Online Curriculum Development workshop in three parts (seminars). The facilitator must be thoroughly familiar with online processes and techniques and be experienced in developing successful curricula. Someone who has taught online and has the skills mentioned adds value to the workshops.

Seminars 1 and 2 should be presented about a week apart to provide assimilation time, as well as time for participants to complete prework. Present Seminar 3 online, using online techniques. No more than 10 people should participate in each seminar. Brief descriptions of the contents of the seminars are included in following sections.

Seminar 1: Introduction to online curriculum development

This seminar reviews characteristics of an online environment; demonstrates a typical online process using a class simulation to replicate activities; reviews and discusses curriculum standards; reviews existing online curriculum packages; and discusses differences between on-ground and online curriculum structures, purposes, and resources involved.

This seminar is presented in four to six hours, and it should include a pre-seminar assignment to be completed for and used in Seminar 2. This assignment should include converting part of a curriculum.

Seminar 2: Facilitative curriculum constructs and tools

This seminar concentrates on structuring a curriculum model, using a selected sample of work brought in by participants in response to the pre-seminar assignment. Small groups modify the selected materials, incorporating construct and tool concepts presented earlier in the class. Intragroup criticism is used, followed by a group review by the seminar facilitator. Participants are asked to finalize their individual curriculum conversion models as a pre-Seminar 3 assignment.

Seminar 3: Critiquing and sharing individual curricula—an online exercise

This seminar is conducted in the online environment and uses an online group process to further develop the individual curriculum packages to production status. Completed packages are submitted to a VC and participants are asked to critique their peer's work. Participants discuss, modify, and sharpen their products in an interactive session spanning about a week. The workshop facilitator further critiques the work, and each participant leaves the last seminar with a completed, production-ready package. A procedure for monitoring the outcome during the first teaching instance with the product also is offered and discussed in this seminar.

Curricula conversion can be taught more than one way. The preceding guidelines provide a way that is proven and can serve as the core of a quality program. It is possible to conduct Seminars 2 and 3 online, and with the right participants, all three seminars could be online.

Q: Secondly, you mention that learning to convert curricula is enhanced by repeated exposure to the facilitative process in VC situations. With that in mind, would it be prudent to ask seasoned instructors to allow potential curricula converters to sit in on classes?

A: Sitting in on classes is one way to improve one's understanding of the differences between the processes, but that option is only productive in environments where the basics are in place: integrated curricula, technologies, and instructors. The strength of an organization from an on-ground perspective is seen by many as all that is needed to achieve the same performance level in an online environment. While current expertise is a great foundation, the differences make online programs a different business, requiring additional skills. Until these skills are achieved, our own internal examples will not necessarily answer your question. One variation on this is to enroll some students in classes at other universities and observe differences in the items noted. This may help.

One more comment: Instructors make good partners in a conversion process. Often they can be the required content experts, but for instructors to be useful in the conversion to online, they must be experienced in online programs. This training can help, but the minimum requirement includes content expertise, facilitative process experience, and familiarization with the online process and environment.

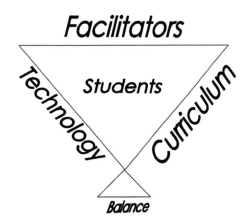

The relationship between curricula, facilitation, and technology

Several times the strong relationships between technology, curriculum, and instructors' skills have been mentioned. We should discuss these relationships in more depth. An example of the impact of these relationships follows.

It is almost impossible to replicate on-ground experience in an online environment, because a different dynamic is at work in a face-to-face experience than in an electronic session. The difference is greatest in a store-and-forward situation, but still significant in an interactive, real-time, electronic interface. (Store-and-forward is asynchronous, allowing students and faculty to send materials to a central consolidation point for distribution to the appropriate addresses. Responses are delayed; students and instructors may not be online at the same time. See Chapter 6 for more detail.)

Several experienced instructors have indicated that an e-mail system, through the Internet, serves their students better than Convene. Our investigation is incomplete, but we can say that the platform shift did not require them to change the design of their curriculum.

Differences in the way we think about curricula become apparent when we consider the two following scenarios:

The on-ground classroom scenario

This is the traditional classroom arrangement, with an instructor in front of the class most of the time. Lecturing is frequent, supplemented by outside study, homework assignments, testing, and in-class exercises such as in small workgroups. The teaching mode can be facilitative or not.

The curriculum is usually semi-structured, with learning objectives, texts, and secondary materials supplied to an instructor. Within the framework provided by these tools, the content expertise of the instructor partially defines the teaching processes for a given class.

The virtual classroom scenario

In this environment, discussions are delayed. Face-to-face contact does not exist. The curriculum is developed to promote dialogue, lectures are few and short, the text is adapted to on-the-job applications, and the instructor becomes a facilitator.

The curriculum development process

The curriculum development process follows generally accepted industry and educational processes. Here, we define the process as a three-step process.

First Step – Define Learning Outcomes.

The learning outcomes will/can be the same as existing outcomes if we are converting existing curriculum from a successful on-ground program.

Second Step – Select the Learning Model to be Used.

There are five choices: interactive, bounded interactive, consultative/interactive, independent/consultative, and a special configuration. These models will be discussed in more detail in a later chapter.

Third Step – Develop the Course Plan.

Defining learning outcomes involves careful consideration of what is to be achieved in the course and in the program if the course is part of an integrated grouping of courses. Learning outcomes provide the basis for all remaining work in developing a piece of curriculum - achieving the outcomes requires that appropriate processes and tools be combined to assure the availability of the essential knowledge to the students.

Selecting the learning model brings in such factors as how many students will be in the VC, what levels of message traffic is to be handled, and how the course will be placed on the learning continuum so synergy plans can be factored into the course design.

After these two steps are initialized, the details can be developed to complete the design.

This process is iterative and will evolve as the process moves forward and reviews are conducted. The process will continue to evolve even as the course is being offered - this will generally be limited to "fine-tuning."

The course plan

Again, the course planning will look familiar to most as it follows basic planning guidelines. Here, we will define course planning as a five-step process.

1. Define and allocate the learning outcomes to the course seminars. Note that the same learning outcome may be seen in more than one seminar within the course - it may take the work done in several seminars to attain the learning outcome.

2. Identify and allocate preparation assignments to the seminars. This includes the background readings, prerequisite exercises, and other activities that may be appropriate to prepare students to process the new information that will be presented in each seminar.

3. Define and allocate long-term assignments and measurements. This includes such course elements as "term papers", progressive case analysis assignments, examinations, and similar items.

4. Identify and apply facilitative support tools, ancillaries, and synergy strategies. This is where the learning outcomes are translated into actual activities and tools and materials assigned to the tasks.

5. Balance the workloads. This is a critical step and involves testing the assignments for do-ability both from the student and facilitator perspectives. This will require an iterative cycle between elements two through four to achieve the correct balance.

A Seminar Development Planning Template for a six-seminar course is included at the end of this chapter. This will assist in tracking the five steps defined above through the completion of the course design.

Check points

Upon completion of the process, one final step is appropriate before attempting the presentation of the course to live students. A complete audit of the key elements should be conducted. The checklist that follows identifies the key elements that should be considered. If possible, the checklist should be applied by someone beside you. This will give additional perspective to the review.

Curriculum Checklist

1. Are the curriculum components compatible with the technologies being used?

2. Is the facilitator's role realistic and doable?

3. Are all learning objectives provided for?

4. Are student expectations clearly defined for each seminar?

5. Do you establish the necessary base knowledge for planned assignments in each seminar?

6. Will the tools selected promote synergy and support required learning?

7. Are assignments doable and reasonable for the educational level being supported?

Socrates© DLTG
Seminar Development Planning Template

	Sem 1	Sem 2	Sem 3	Sem 4	Sem 5	Sem 6
Learning Objectives						
Prep Assignments						
Long Term Assignments						
Support Tools						
Balance						

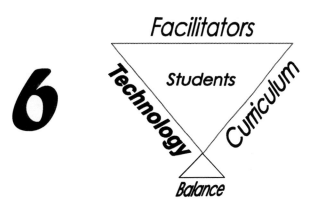

6

The Technology

Online technology is intended to be low profile and is used as a tool in the learning process. Many delivery systems exist, including Internet interfaces, privately customized software, and direct dial access. Technical hardware includes private servers, IPs (Internet providers), and space leased from software providers.

The availability of customer service is a major concern in choosing software and hardware, and good customer service is always a factor in the success of a program. Students and facilitators must be able to log online and use the software as intended. Primary considerations in making technological decisions include:

- ◆ computer and network support (internal or external)
- ◆ training for students and faculty
- ◆ technical support (helpline) for students

- software platforms (DOS, Win 3.1, Win 95, Macintosh, etc.)

- applications software (standardized or free choice; especially important to curriculum development)

- the Internet/Web

While many elements should be considered in developing and implementing a technical delivery strategy, a critical relationship exists between a user friendly student

> *To succeed, you must have a user-friendly student interface and a reliable and available system.*

interface and a reliable and available system on the one hand, and the success or failure of a program on the other. If the technology is unreliable and difficult to use, the system will fail.

Several variations of software and distance learning models are used today. The asynchronous online model uses store-and-forward technology, which makes possible the following advantages:

- private mailboxes for participants

- a common area where all invited participants can read messages

- branch meetings within a primary meeting

Messages are sent and stored until the intended addressee signs on and requests the messages. Though similar, this is different than an electronic mail system.

The feel of the VC is very much like being in a physical classroom. The obvious difference is that you are not sitting in a traditional classroom listening to a lecture. The process is interactive and requires the attention of all participants.

Signing on and finding 10 to 20 messages is not unusual; if you miss a day, you may have twice that much. While not every message is responded to by every person, participants should read and consider all messages. Store-and-forward technology allows a maximum degree of flexibility.

In the diagram of the various program configurations in the Socrates portfolio, you may not notice much difference between models at first. After carefully considering each option, you will see that tradeoffs exist.

In the asynchronous online model:

◆ You can see a picture of the person to whom you are sending a note.

◆ The classroom is open 24 hours a day, seven days a week.

◆ You are not required to be online at any specific time to communicate with others.

◆ Equipment needs are minimal.

◆ The mode of communication is flexible.

◆ Responses to communications are delayed (usually up to 24 hours).

◆ Potential markets are restricted only by the need to access a computer, a modem, and a telephone line.

In the synchronous model:

◆ You may or may not see a picture in real time of the person with whom you are communicating.

◆ Specific equipment can be required for any option.

◆ The Internet, special telephone services, and TV links are the mode of communication.

- The expense of operating in real time can be significant.

- Participants must be in a specific place at a specific time.

- Potential markets are restricted due to difficulties in operating in a synchronous mode (crossing international datelines, time zone constraints, etc.).

Expenses vary from model to model, and customer support, customer service, and reliability issues differ among models. For instance, consider the case of the major national Internet provider that was unable to provide adequate telephone access to its customers. An online program connected through that provider would be unusable. The article "Earn a Masters, Virtually" reveals a variety of technological options available today.

Different organizations and programs require different supportive services. User friendly and reliable technology is vital. A student or faculty member who cannot function on the system will drag the entire program down. Prompt service must be available. For these reasons, the program discussed in this course will be the asynchronous online model.

Technology and the educational process

No.	Entity	Technology	Program	Scope	Notes
1.	Baker College	asynchronous online	academic	national	Students use CD-ROMs to run demonstrations and conduct lab exercises.
2.	IKON Corp.	asynchronous online	technical certification	national	
3.	THEN	asynchronous online	professional certification	international	Students use intranet to communicate while off campus. Students meet on campus every other weekend and for a week in the summer. Group and individual projects are completed using the Intranet as a communications platform.
4.	Vanderbilt University	intranet	MBA	regional	
5.	Colorado State University	asynchronous online hybrid	MBA	international	Class lectures are video taped on-ground and shipped to students. The online element is used to post information.
6.	Bill Riley	Convene elec. conferencing	personal improvement	international	Students meet for eight one-hour electronic sessions to learn high-yield vegetable gardening.

					Professors post lectures on the Internet, students dialogue in chat rooms, and lessons are sent via e-mail.
7.	New School	Internet/ synchronous online	various grad degrees	national	
8.	JEC College Connection	TV, e-mail, video, Internet, satellite	undergrad/ grad/cert	regional	Courses are offered using combinations of media. Videos are sold to the student.
9.	University of Alaska	e-mail, online chat	undergrad/ various	national	
10.	Regents College, NY	e-mail, online chat, discussion boards	undergrad/ grad/various	national	
11.	Thomas Edison State, NJ	mail, e-mail, brief residence	graduate	national	
12.	EUN	mail, e-mail, message boards, proctored exams	various	national	
13.	Knowledge Online	video lectures, e-mail, fax	various	national	

Selection criteria for technology

In recent years, a convergence of telecommunications, computing, and audiovisual capabilities has emerged in the distance learning industry. Telephone services are changing from analog to digital, and sound, photos, graphics, and videos can be stored digitally as well. This allows many new options in selecting tools and software. Sophisticated satellite links to e-mail systems create even more options. In considering which technology would best meet the needs of a

> *The convergence of telecommunications, computing, and audiovisual capabilities creates many possibilities for tools and software.*

given application, several factors must be considered, including those in the following list. The considerations listed in this section not only demonstrate the importance of a system that is easy to use, but also how training should be accomplished.

♦ Ease of use

Students and faculty members must understand and be able to use a technology. Knowing the skill level required to use a given technology can help in selecting a delivery system. The more sophisticated a technology is, the more critical the ease-of-use issue becomes. A technology that is sophisticated enough to be easy for students and instructors to use can also be so sophisticated that the same people cannot solve technical problems that arise from the technology.

To illustrate this point, consider VCRs. Some inexpensive VCRs have only one function: play, and so they are easy to operate. But in addition to playing recorded videos, many people buy VCRs to record movies and other television programming, even when they are not home. Why, then, do many never learn to use anything

> *Experience has shown that hands-on training is very effective in teaching the use of technology.*

more than the play function? The owner's manual explains the other functions and how to use them, but most people find manuals difficult to understand, and they don't want to spend the time to figure out how to use these functions by experimenting with the equipment.

People avoid education, sometimes because of the medium (e.g., printed manuals). This tendency can be seen in the following example. A group of business executives talking about cellular telephones revealed that although most cellular phones are capable of much more than placing calls, that is all they use them for. Many said they could not take the time to read and comprehend the manual. Value-added services and products will not bring a higher price than less sophisticated offerings if consumers (users) cannot understand the features or use them in real-world settings. This is worth considering in your selection criteria.

♦ Training students and faculty members to use a technology

Experience has shown that hands-on training is very effective in teaching the use of technology. Many software providers provide interactive CDs, interactive training programs downloaded from the net, and training formats that allow students to learn to use technologies in a setting that replicates the use of the software in a learning environment. In addition to training students and faculty members to use the technology, it is important to realize that problems with technologies do occur. When these problems arise, someone must be able to respond quickly. Distance learners do not want to be inconvenienced by technological problems. Consider in your technology selection how much training will be required to teach someone to assist students with their problems and who will fix the big problems.

> *The technology must be adaptable to the changing needs of students and the institution.*

♦ Total costs of the technology including setup, distribution, maintenance, upgrades, and use

The choice of a medium, the existing infrastructure, the space required, and the supportive technology must be considered in determining setup costs, which can be as little as a few hundred dollars or as much as several millions of dollars. Systems requiring direct lines to each learning site, satellite links, and supportive features that allow synchronous activities are costly and can take years to implement. In learning models requiring the distribution of materials, you must consider the means, the reliability of the means, and the costs of providing the service. Software, kits, text, and other supportive materials must be distributed in a reliable and predictable manner. The number of vendors used to supply these materials and whether or not the materials will be shipped to a central location for distribution will affect the cost. The technology you select and the supporting structures must be maintained. The cost of maintaining your system can be anywhere from nothing to an amount so large that maintenance costs become the most important single factor in whether or not you can use the technology

Programs change and so do markets. A technology that is adaptable to the changing needs of students and the institution is important. An institution's vision can change in a distance learning environment. Once under way, distance learning providers often discover that market possibilities are greater than they expected. Also, new

> *Service and reliability are key aspects of attracting and maintaining a customer base.*

programs with new enhancements emerge constantly. Adapting to these new offerings is crucial. The ability to upgrade your system or change it in other ways can be a necessity in some situations. Always know the capabilities and the limitations of a given technology.

♦ The availability of the technology and supportive systems

Knowing the availability of existing options is critical. If your program is Internet-based, your service area is restricted to areas with Internet service. If you use an online program via a direct dial access system, your customers will need a phone line. Who will provide support and what is the availability of the support structure? If an institution is using a software provider's servers as a technology base, what is the availability of support to customers? These are all elements you must explore.

♦ The cost to students of meeting technological requirements

Your students' financial ability to meet the technical requirements of a given technology can be significant. One might expect that the average college student who owns a computer has Windows and a CD-ROM drive installed and no less than 16MB of RAM. If you base key technological decisions on assumptions like this one, your market is limited to only those who can afford these capabilities.

Of 1,400 students enrolled in one of the nation's largest distance learning programs, only 400 had Windows capabilities; 1,000 were still using MS-DOS. Know the capabilities of those you wish to serve; surprises belong to those who make assumptions. If students cannot afford to upgrade to the technology you employ, they are lost as customers.

♦ System support (e.g., help desk, technical, utilities)

Whether a problem is perceived or real, it must be resolved in a timely and proficient manner. Consider this one of the most critical aspects of maintaining your customer base. The reputation, credibility, and ability of an institution to retain customers rests on this aspect. Frustration runs high when busy people spend money on a program that professes to be convenient and reliable but does not deliver. Sometimes, an institution does not get a second chance. Negative word-of-mouth has a powerful effect on the market; therefore, it is better to err on the side of caution when estimating these costs and your prospective students' ability to pay them. Competition is always growing, and service and reliability are key aspects of attracting and maintaining a customer base.

♦ The ability of the technology to meet the goals and the desired outcomes of the program

The institution offering a distance learning program must understand what it is trying to do, the programs it will offer, the expected gain in using technology to deliver a program, what standards are set and understood, how the performance of the technology will be measured, and the role of technology in achieving the goals. Be specific and precise about your expectations of the technology. Consider every aspect from the curriculum changes that may be required to the training required to use a given technology. If the technology will not meet every requirement as expected, either the technology must be changed or the processes, goals, and expectations must be changed.

♦ The cost to the student

All costs associated with a distance learning program are going to be paid by someone. Knowing the cost implications of a given technology is important. If your customers cannot afford the program fees resulting from a given selection of technology, you cannot afford to use that technology. This sounds like basic business, but many fail to realize its importance. Thinking that supercharged technology will create a market in itself is instant failure. The question is, how selective do you want the program to be, based on the technology alone?

Careful consideration of these factors can save an organization time, money, and frustration. The technology selected should accommodate the lowest common denominator. The need for ease of use and accessibility to service cannot be overstated. The costs, goals, and market should be well understood before selecting a technology.

Technological options and associated characteristics

Basic equipment for the asynchronous online model

Participants are connected to a virtual classroom (server) via direct dial access or via the Internet. This requires the students to have a computer, a phone line, a modem, and an Internet Provider (if connecting via the Internet). Using direct dial access, a student's system is connected to the server directly through the phone line via modem. No other interface (other than the phone system) is necessary for the connection. Physically, a virtual classroom consists of the student's system and a server that is used to store, sort, and forward messages. Connection is made from the student's system through a modem to another modem and into the server. Data coming to the student's system is transported via the connection initiated by the student. It is simple in terms of today's technology, but very effective.

Students also can access the system via the Internet. Using the Internet, the student is connected to the primary server (the VC) after connecting with the Internet provider. Most Internet providers operate by managing many phone lines, controlled by electronic equipment that connects the student to a series of servers covering the globe. These servers contain the addresses and linking framework needed to connect to the various web sites that exist around the world.

The Internet provider estimates the demand for telephone line use over a given period of time. For example, the Internet provider has 10,000 customers that use the services, but estimates that only 1,900 customers will dial in to the system at any given time. The provider then purchases a T-1 or T-3 (a set of high quality dedicated phone lines) that will handle 1,900 calls. The controller used by the Internet provider automatically connects customers to lines when they are available. If the Internet provider receives 2,700 calls at one time, 800 calls will receive busy signals.

Another factor to consider is that the bandwidth (the amount of data the phone line will carry) is much greater in the T-1 and T-3 dedicated lines than in the line running to the student's home. A broader bandwidth allows video, audio, and real-time events to take place through the Internet connection easily. (That is, the lines have room to carry massive data files.) Currently, this capacity is limited with direct dial access to a site. The quality of the messages you receive depends on the capabilities of the student's system and the phone lines that connect it to the Internet provider. Just because your IP has a broad bandwidth does not necessarily mean that the phone lines to your home are of the same quality or that they will transport data quickly and clearly.

Let's look at some of the characteristics of distance learning programs that are using different technologies, beginning with the asynchronous online model using a direct dial access:

Characteristics of required hardware

Institution providing program: server, modem, telephone lines, and computer. This structure can be provided through the software provider, leaving the institution to deal with none of this. Monthly fees are based on students per month.

Participating student or facilitator: modem, telephone line, and computer. The student or facilitator can use a system where they work or at home, or systems may be provided by an institution.

Ease of use: Facilitators and students can be trained to use the technology in one week (given a low level of computer knowledge).

Time to implement: 30 to 60 days, including training instructors and students and converting or developing the curriculum.

Cost: a facilitator or student can purchase the technology required for under $1,000, including the computer.

Institution: If the institution is going to purchase hardware to administer the program, the cost will depend on the number of students. A general setup figure for the purchase of servers, computers, phone lines, and modems is approximately $25,000. If the institution chooses to use a software provider's system, the cost can be between $7 and $25 per participant, per month (including an 800 direct dial access number). Initial software for students will cost between nothing and $100. Institutions providing the server base for the program must account for all variable, fixed, and mixed costs associated with operating the system, i.e., power, space, service, support staff, upgrades, depreciation, phone lines, etc.

If students use the Internet as a connection, an Internet provider cost will be incurred. A typical phone bill for a student participating in an online program that does not offer an 800 service is in the range of $20 a month. Internet provider costs range from $16 a month for unlimited use to pay-by-the-minute options (if you can get on for a minute). The connection time on average for an online asynchronous participant is 20 to 45

> *Distance learning is moving from a national scale to include foreign educational markets.*

seconds per call. The average Internet connection times run approximately five to 30 hours per month, depending on the program and individual chat.

The characteristics of current distance learning technologies

Computers and technologies change and evolve at an ever-increasing rate. The rate at which these technologies are incorporated by educational institutions is much slower. Because of this, we can look at the technologies in use today and speculate as to the evolution of distance learning technology. Distance learning today is practiced on a national scale. This is changing, and inroads are being made in foreign educational markets. Companies such as Embanet and schools such as Colorado State University have students in 13 countries as well as all 50 states. National providers of distance education are emerging as pioneers of global education. Therefore, it makes sense to study the technologies in use today and to assess and better understand the benefits and limitations of various technologies for use in global education.

The three broad categories of technologies in use today are text-based systems, audio systems, and the World Wide Web.

Text-based systems

These include e-mail, muds and moos, computer conferencing, real-time chat, and many uses of Web-based audio and video conferencing.

Real-time and asynchronous applications are available today in integrated seamless formats. This implies that video, audio, and text can be accessed within the same operating platform (see Centra Symposium on the World Wide Web). Moos (multi-object-oriented) are a text-based virtual reality development from muds (multi-user dungeons used in playing dungeons and dragons). Moos allow the manipulation of and interaction with cyber objects as part of the communication process. When integrated into the learning experience, moos can be used to create an environment in which students interact more directly with course ideas than they might in an unstructured discussion.

Text-based systems can be divided according to whether they are primarily synchronous or asynchronous. The technologies usually support both formats, but one or the other is the primary intended format. The format influences the design of interactive features. In supporting students, text-based systems are usually used to deliver course contents and provide a medium of interaction in an asynchronous model. Discussions and activities are primary elements in achieving the learning objectives in an asynchronous environment.

Various instructional and conceptual tools designed to stimulate dialogue are used in asynchronous learning process. They include but are not limited to discussion questions, polarization of issues, case studies, lectures, presentations, guest speakers, and team projects. In addition, various informational and media tools are used as supportive elements. This technology has been used successfully over the last ten years in large scale operations and has tremendous potential for overseas use, given current levels of communications technologies.

> *It is critical to understand how a technology will impact an organization, the students, the facilitator, and the learning process.*

Successful asynchronous text-based programs exist at an international level. They include technical certifications, MBA programs, import/export certification courses, and second language teaching. Another text-based advantage of asynchronous learning models is that people worldwide can access these programs at home with a phone line and personal computer.

Many arguments have been made concerning asynchronous text-based programs. The equalizing effects of textual communication is one, and the concentration on what is said rather than who says it is another. Judgmental reactions to the physically challenged are removed in the text-based format. Text-based systems do not remove bias and advantage; they merely shift it. Those with no financial limitations can use state-of-the-art systems more freely and participate (for example, from both work and home) without concern for the cost. These people have the advantage in terms of being able to participate in discussions more easily than those for whom the costs are restrictive.

Those who are better at communicating in writing may dominate in terms of the number and quality of messages sent, but people whose writing skills are not as developed learn from the expertise of others. The freedom to choose one's time and place for interacting allows students to think through their viewpoints before submitting ideas or opinions in the VC. Students making their opinions known, responding to other viewpoints, and engaging in dialogue are critical to learning outcomes. A person unable to keep up with the flow of the discussions tends to be at a disadvantage. These people must be advised by the facilitator concerning their participation level. The system will be as flawed as the human beings who use it. Nevertheless, for some groups of people, text-based interaction allows access to education in a form to which they are ideally suited.

Audio systems

Audio conferencing over ordinary telephone lines is a low tech solution to supporting students around the world, due to the telephone's widespread use. Text-based distance education programmers use audio conferencing to help motivate students, and it has also been used for small group collaborative work. Few uses exist for this technology in asynchronous text-based models. Audio conferences are difficult to manage and place new requirements on students and facilitators, including simultaneous attendance.

Audiographics, which consists of voice plus a shared screen for drawing or sharing prepared graphics, is available in several software packages. As with audio conferencing, audiographics used among more than two sites necessitates an audio bridge to connect all the lines. Internationally, cost is the limiting factor. Some systems use the Internet the carry data; others use ISDN (integrated services digital network), a set of international switching standards to which adherence is recommended to worldwide telecommunications providers.

Audio over the Internet is an emerging technology, which a number of educational institutions are developing with the Internet as the medium. Real-time audio, for example, is a product that allows real-time lectures on a global scale (see http://www.realaudio.com); international connections are slow in handling two-way communications. Internet products like Real Audio make it possible for large numbers of students to access broadcasts in real or delayed time.

Video systems are costly, and many educators do not think they are necessary to provide a quality distance learning experience. Many do not think video is necessary to support students at a distance and that audiographics works better, because the focus is on the content of the material. Justifying the significantly higher cost of including a video component in a course, in relation to the educational benefits, can be difficult, given the mostly text-based nature of the courses. But many feel video contributes to motivation and social aspects and facilitates delivery of higher quality learning materials.

One-way video (with two-way audio) systems are used frequently. Many of these systems use satellite delivery to extend coverage. Lecture at a distance with students in remote sites is a primary format with this technology. Video conferencing is used in this format for long distance communications.

Two-way video conferencing over ISDN is replacing one-way systems. Global standards concerning the interoperability of ISDN systems are still problematic. International point-to-point and even multi-point videoconferences take place daily in the workplace and are relatively frequent occurrences among educational institutions. The cost of this mode of communication is a significant issue.

PictureTel has designed a video conferencing system specifically for the education market (http://www.picturetel.com) called Socrates. Socrates is an integrated presentation station with a touch-sensitive screen that allows a lecturer to see on one window of the lectern exactly what is being shown to students locally and remotely, and on another window, to preview visual aids prepared for the lecture or to browse remote sites.

Streaming video on the Internet is another developing technology, technically feasible today, but restricted by the bandwidth available internationally. In theory this allows images to be downloaded by remote sites in real time. Video clips integrated into text-based material to illustrate and highlight are more commonly used today.

The World Wide Web

The Web facilitates most media. Text and text-based interaction, audio and video clips, multi-way interactive audio media video as clips, and multi-way interactive audio/video are all used via the Web. The Web is an awesome means of providing education; its applications in global education are significant. The Internet is not universal, and not everyone can access the net. Today's IP must be studied carefully in terms of reliability and availability, but the Web is a means of accessing millions of addresses.

The Web has three defining characteristics:

- the use of URLs (universal resource locators), which provide the addressing system

- the HTTP standard (Hypertext Transfer Protocol), by which requested information is delivered

- the development of HTML (Hypertext Markup Language), through which links are made between documents and parts of documents

The Web was developed from a client-server architecture. Customers access the server and tell it where to go and what to get; the server does it, terminates the connection, and proceeds to serve the next customer. This procedure allows a server to handle many thousands of customer requests per day.

Customers can use the Web to download programs, course information, and the software to run the program. All software upgrades and maintenance can be downloaded by the customer automatically via the Web. This is an ease-of-use factor that was discussed earlier.

Understanding how a given technology will impact an organization, the students, the facilitator, and the learning process is critical to the success of a program. These issues are understood through planning, information gathering, experience, and professionals who are a solidly grounded in the industry. Spending the time to understand, up front, will eliminate many troublesome problems.

Platforms used in online learning today

Text-based systems are commonly used in distance learning programs today. The largest, fastest growing, and most successful programs use only a few software packages: Convene, Embanet, and Lotus Notes. Convene and Embanet are the most widely used software packages. The University of Phoenix and Baker College offer two of the biggest and most recognized programs. Both institutions use Convene as primary software. Colorado State University uses the web-based Embanet as its primary software.

Convene

Convene is a group communications program that provides a means for users to meet people who share their interests. Convene's features include:

♦ flexibility in creating meetings

- meeting access controlled by invitation

- special request features that allow specific information and lists to be generated

- short connection time, usually seconds

- viewing of notes and files without leaving Convene, using viewers

- requires a 386 or more powerful system with 8MB of RAM and a modem

- MS-DOS, Microsoft Windows 3.1, Microsoft Windows 95, and Macintosh platforms can participate

- only one week software training from your location

- low cost

- use of Convene's servers or your own

- customer support

- access via direct dial or the Internet

- permission to copy Convene disks for personal use by others but not for sale

- 800 number access, reducing the cost to the student

Convene is used in the asynchronous learning model. The model involves balancing the technology with the facilitation process and the curriculum. Typically the facilitator will upload course information with assignments, projects, and reading requirements. Students who are invited to the meeting sign onto the system and receive the materials. The learning process is designed to stimulate dialogue among students. Both Convene and Embanet are credible distance learning providers that use this model.

Companies use Convene to provide certification courses and corporate training. The learning model most commonly used with Convene allows tremendous flexibility. The classroom is open 24 hours a day, seven days a week. Students in the VC are typically expected to sign onto the VC five of seven days a week, thus students see responses to questions and concerns within 24 hours. The process allows the facilitator to monitor the learning process or participate in the interaction daily.

> *The classroom is open 24 hours a day, seven days a week.*

Because of the intense interaction and the rapid rate at which information is assimilated, distance learning courses are frequently completed in much less time than in a traditional classroom. In support of achieving the learning objectives, many programs include CD-ROMs or videotapes to provide interactive lab exercises, visual aids, and class demonstrations.

Embanet

Embanet provides a web-based campus model for learning that can be used in an asynchronous or synchronous mode. Embanet features include:

- real-time floating chat rooms
- global access
- course administration and testing without need of facilitator intervention
- internal and external e-mail systems
- conferencing without requiring HTML programming or e-mail distribution lists
- message history tracking
- multi-level security features
- encryption protected file transfers
- database access to many value-added features
- low cost
- complete customization and administration services
- strong customer service
- downloading software to students' systems via the Internet
- interactive software training via the Internet

Colorado State University uses Embanet to ship videotaped on-ground lectures to supplement the learning process. The learning model facilitates a hundred or more students in each class. The program at CSU has been in service over 10 years.

The following table contrasts the profiles of the two software packages.

ELEMENT	EMBANET	CONVENE
Internet accessed	Y	Y
security	Y	Y
asynchronous	Y	Y
synchronous	Y	N
customer support	Y	Y
IP required	Y	N
direct dial access	N	Y
low cost	Y	Y
proven system	Y	Y
Global access	Y	Y
Ease of use	Y	Y
Aggressive upgrades	Y	Y
Software training at your location	Y	Y

Other considerations

In providing a utility grade service to customers, the accessibility of reliable and cost-effective IPs is a consideration.

Real-time and asynchronous applications are available today in integrated seamless formats. This implies that video, audio, and text can be accessed within the same operating platform. Programs such as the Centra Symposium are web-based and offer many options for the distance learning paradigm. In selecting a technology platform and distance learning process, value-added and non-value-added elements should be considered. Do the learning outcomes require video, audio, or both? What are the benefits in relation to the costs?

Costs change in relation to the factors below, as well as other factors.

◆ equipment required by the customer and the institution

◆ training required to use the software effectively

◆ maintenance activities

◆ upgrade activities

◆ support staff requirements

◆ reliability functions

◆ availability functions

◆ infrastructure

◆ software capability

Each element within the technological framework of a distance learning model carries with it problems. Problems can include servers crashing, modems failing, IPs failing to perform, telephone line troubles, and software that will not load properly. All successful programs respond quickly and effectively to problems. Customers' expectations are high in distance learning programs, and failure of the institution to perform will result in a loss of customers.

Focus on the programs to be offered. What are the required learning outcomes? What are the standards? What technology elements are necessary to facilitate the learning process? Think about ways to adapt the curriculum, tools that can be used, the capabilities of the students and faculty members, and how it all fits together. More is not always better in this paradigm. Many facilitators see no use for video or audio in text-based asynchronous programs. The benefits identified are usually offset by the significant costs associated with the setup, maintenance, and support of the features.

Market considerations are important when selecting a technology package. Technology changes faster than the market can assimilate the changes. MS-DOS is still used on lower end systems by large numbers of distance learning students and facilitators every day. If these people are not desired as customers, then no consideration is needed. Baker College does not think this way, because as mentioned previously, 1000 of their 1400 online students still use MS-DOS on lower end systems.

When considering the scope and context of potential foreign markets, basic services can be major considerations. In synchronous programs, the ability of the customer to commit to being in one place at a given time is a factor to be considered. Several programs require residencies, adding additional demands to a learning process that should accommodate the customer. Demands placed on customers may be necessary to achieve the learning objectives of the program, or they may not. Careful consideration must be given to every aspect in deciding how to offer a program. Every limiting factor reduces the potential market.

Facilitators

Technology _Students_ _Curriculum_

Balance

7

Program Models and Tools

Introduction

In the chapter titled _How Many Students Make a Class?_, a relationship is defined between the dialogue level and the number of students that can be managed appropriately (see the following chart). The number of students in a class becomes a critical element in the design of curriculum since the economics of the program relate to the class size. At the same time, in many—even most—cases, an important consideration is the dialogue activity among the students and between the students and the facilitator.

Maintaining a balance in the virtual classroom is key to providing a positive learning experience for all involved. If the combination of activities we select to present a subject is misdirected, we face the possibility of unreasonable demands on students and facilitators, boring dialogue, the encouragement of drift from the subject matter, and many of the other pitfalls of improper design balance.

Program Model Summary

Number of Students per Class	Applicable Model	Design Dialogue Levels per Student	
10-15	Interactive	10-12 messages per week	Interactive
15-25	Bounded interactive	5-8 messages per week	Interactive
25-40	Consultative/ interactive	2-5 messages per week	Reduced interactivity
40-60	Independent/ consultative	Student-facilitator-student only	Non-interactive
Above 60	Special configuration	Varies with design	Special

A successful curriculum design applies a number of carefully selected tools to the learning situation to achieve the learning outcomes. The tools can be used in several ways; this chapter will look at them from the view of their role in generating

> *A successful curriculum design applies a number carefully selected tools to the learning situation to achieve the learning outcomes.*

or controlling the level of dialogue that takes place in the virtual environment. The solution ultimately is a system solution with the tools acting in concert with other control parameters to meet the needs of the situation.

This chapter will look at the four specific models, plus special case models for online learning. It will also define tools that will assist in creating sound curriculum.

Models

In this classification, we have two models: the interactive model and the bounded interactive model.

The interactive model

The base model for online education is the **interactive model**. As shown in the chart below, the model limits class size to 15 or fewer students and requires a minimum of seven to eight students.

The reason for these limits is the dependence on a high level of dialogue to achieve the goals of this model. We incorporate specific tools to create the desired level of dialogue in the model while keeping the environment focused on achieving the learning outcomes. We use these tools to create a level of control in the environment to do several things, including:

- achieving the learning outcomes defined for the course or workshop

- maintaining a level of dialogue between students that is productive and does not unreasonably load the students

- keeping the composite dialogue activity at a level that can be processed by the facilitator

The control parameters noted do not just apply to the interactive model; it applies to all models. And the tool content for the course will vary with the model. As the chart implies, we can handle only a limited amount of dialogue before we must depend on other tools to produce the desired results. As a rule of thumb, when the message rate exceeds 200 messages per workshop, we are reaching the limit at which students and facilitators can be expected to function comfortably. So if we limit our online tool kit to dialogue, we would limit class size to that of the interactive model.

The following table illustrates this scenario.

Interactive Model

Parameters	Tools
High level of discussion	Discussion questions
Desirable in socially oriented courses. HR. etc.	Small group activities
	Subject papers
	Article critiques
	Interview sharing
	Directed dialogue

In the initial implementations of online programs, this limit was accepted. Very good programs developed around these parameters, but the economics always have been marginal. As interest expands to better economic performance and a broadened scope of subject matter, other models emerge.

The bounded interactive model

The first to be considered was the **bounded interactive** model. This model only slightly relaxed the dialogue requirements. The control mechanism for this is to increase the group or independent study content to reduce the discussion that takes place in the virtual classroom. This adjustment allows increased class size without seriously compromising the objectives.

The following table illustrates this model.

Bounded Interactive Model

Parameters	Tools
High level of discussion needed, but can be limited	Discussion questions
Courses with technical content, mathematics, etc.	Group activities
	Group subject papers
	Article critiques
	Interview sharing
	Directed dialogue

Requests to provide classes with higher levels of technical content began to appear in the online curriculum programs. When the student, content, curriculum, and facilitator characteristics are considered, it is evident that more independent study content can be included in such programs. This is because the materials to be studied need to be heavily grounded in theory before discussions can be approached logically. The students in technical programs often are less attracted to situations where they must dialogue; they prefer to study and respond independently. The facilitators available for many of the technical courses are content experts with only a limited exposure to teaching or facilitator skills. Thus, effective curricula can include limited group activities, workbooks, independent laboratory experiments, video viewing, and other such tools. Each of these tools can be used effectively to reduce the levels of discussion without losing course content.

Reduced interactivity model

In the **Consultative/Interactive** model, tools that require independent effort are incorporated and the level of dialogue is reduced to very low levels in favor of independent activities and small group projects. The facilitator assumes the role of a consultant to the individuals and group projects. This reduces the workload involved for a higher number of students while still providing significant value added in the online process. This model is extremely good where there can be a high content of programmed learning involved. Workbooks, interactive CD-ROM sessions, definitive case studies and other such medium are useful in these models.

This model includes the key features shown in the following table.

Consultative/Interactive Model

Parameters	Tools
Extreme limits on interactivity	Definitive case studies
Desirable in technically oriented courses	Text
	Web activities
	CD-ROM
	Workbooks
	Video
	Activity kits

The non-interactive model

The **Independent/Consultative** model uses the online capability for moving assignments and responses between the student and the facilitator. Administrative activities also can be handled online, making the total process suitable for serving students who are not on a campus. No student-to-student interaction is planned in the curriculum; only a limited level of facilitator involvement is included. In fact, the instructor is much more like a faculty person than a facilitator. As mentioned earlier, this model is directed at being more of an electronic means of monitoring an independent study course.

The characteristics of this model are given in the following table.

Independent/Consultative Model

Parameters	Tools
No or low levels of discussion Desirable in non-socially oriented courses	Subject papers Definitive case studies Critiques Interviews Essays Testing

Is online effective in the non-interactive models?

As we reduce the level of interactivity in our models, the question of value added comes to the front. When you reach a point where the online component is only sending and receiving messages, would it be more effective to move to the more traditional correspondence course model where everything is written and passed to the instructor via regular mail?

Institutions will come down on both sides of this discussion. Generally, however, the question will be "Which mail system will we use, the post office or electronic mail, to move our materials to students

working in very low or non-interactive models?"
Within these boundaries, we can use fast turn-
around services such as UPS, proprietary electronic
mail systems, or the Internet. Remember, the
technologies used for interactive models is more
than just mail; it includes many editing and control
procedures that facilitate handling of large
quantities of messages, usually associated with
dialogue-type models. The cost of the electronic
alternatives range from reasonable to nearly zero;
increasingly, the answer is still electronic mail of
some sort.

Special models

Many possible combinations can be formed by
varying the features and tools used in the preceding
models. This offers a method for fine-tuning the
models to meet the particular needs of an
institution, program, course, or accreditation body.

It also is possible to use model variations to handle
larger class sizes. The following diagram illustrates
a model that can be used for several hundred
students located in several locations worldwide.

Multi-Site Large Audience Model

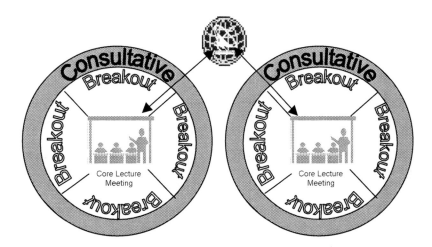

- ◆ There can be as many locations as desired.

- ◆ Each core site can have several hundred participants.

- ◆ Each breakout should have around 25 students. The number of breakouts is determined by the number of students served in the core site.

- ◆ The breakouts are serviced by teaching assistants.

- ◆ The consultative ring is staffed by a subject expert(s) and is done online.

The basic model design was used in a proposal for an institution that wanted to use satellite links to distribute a central message to multiple locations worldwide. They then wanted to form breakout groups led by teaching assistants to further develop the course materials. Students were given assignments to complete at home as a continuing part of the course. As follow-up, the consultative ring was formed as an online service to students as a means of continuing support until the course assignments were completed. There are options for multiple cycles of this process for complex programs that will cover weeks or months. The same model could easily be adapted to a one-time course or seminar format.

This model can be adapted to operate as a large single-site classroom with the breakout sections being independent study groups that report on assignments to the central facilitator as a group (not individually). The number of breakouts can be as many as 10 to 15, with 10 to 15 student members each, totaling 100 to 200 students under the guidance of one facilitator.

Access to the facilitator is very limited and generally is restricted to submitting completed project segments for grading and comment. The facilitator can be viewed as actually handling the equivalent of 10 to 15 students in this model.

The outer consulting ring can be a group of consultant/subject area specialists that are accessible to the breakout groups for special assistance on a controlled, but liberal basis.

In this design, the curriculum design is particularly important and the materials provided to the groups are equally significant. Complex case studies are good candidates for this process. The model will soon be used in an Executive MBA program with a single progressive case being used as the prevailing activity for the overall MBA program.

If assistants are added to the breakout group construct, a model constructed in this manner can facilitate large numbers of students in highly interactive processes. As an alternative, the model can be used where little to no interactivity is required. This variation provides for a range of interaction options while allocating only the teaching/support facilitator requirements that are absolutely necessary for the intended outcomes.

Tools

Tools are the processes, techniques, software, events, and other means applied to learning situations to achieve desired learning outcomes with a specific level of activity or interaction. Online tools are to be selected carefully during the curriculum planning stage. The application and combination of tools prescribed by the facilitator or curriculum designer drive the process to the desired conclusions. Most tools would apply to on-ground learning situations also.

The following is a list of useful online tools:

- Activity kits
- Assignment pacing
- Audio files
- Brainstorming
- Case study/analysis
- CD-ROM ancillaries
- Chat sessions (real-time)
- Class projects
- Current article critiques
- Debates
- Dialogue control

- ♦ Essays
- ♦ Experience sharing
- ♦ Focused reports
- ♦ Group activities
- ♦ Group discussion questions (open or closed)
- ♦ Group subject papers
- ♦ Guest lectures
- ♦ Independent assignments
- ♦ Independent laboratory experiments
- ♦ Individual discussion questions (open or closed)
- ♦ Interviews
- ♦ Lecturettes
- ♦ Online libraries
- ♦ Polarized challenge
- ♦ Research
- ♦ Simulations
- ♦ Subject papers
- ♦ Surveys
- ♦ Team projects
- ♦ Term projects
- ♦ Testing
- ♦ Textbook discussion
- ♦ Video files
- ♦ Video tapes
- ♦ Voting
- ♦ Web activities
- ♦ Web search exercises
- ♦ Web site visits

- Weekly summary critiques
- Workbooks
- Workplace exchanges

In summary

The online learning paradigm is proving useful for a multitude of applications that range from highly technical training in a non-interactive learning model to a marketing management class in a highly interactive learning model. From seven people locally to 200 or more people in an international training program, online learning models are available to successfully meet the challenges of many corporate and academic needs for the 21st century. The key to using these models is the application and combination of tools to drive the process to the desired conclusions.

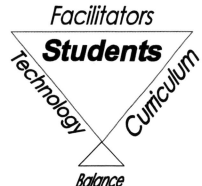

How Many Students Make a Class?

Introduction

In the simplest terms, a cost evaluation of offering an online class involves subtracting the cost of providing the class from the product of the number of students, multiplied by the amount of tuition charged. Administrators are interested in holding down fixed costs while enrolling as many students as feasible in class in order to achieve their financial goals.

Successful financial outcomes are different to different people. Minimizing tuition for students is usually a concern, and achieving high profit margins is usually attractive, but regardless of these priorities, the more students accommodated in each class, the better the likelihood of reaching financial goals.

Pay attention to two factors when designing an online course. You want to:

- achieve the learning objectives
- maintain a realistic level of activity among students and the facilitator

Our approach to meeting these requirements influences the number of students that can be supported in a VC. This chapter focuses on the factors that affect financial outcomes and ways that each factor influences the number of students in a class.

Level of dialogue

Dialogue level refers to the number of messages sent by students and facilitator during a given time period.

> *Dialogue is a major source of learning in a virtual classroom.*

What makes it possible to support more, or less, students in a class? The dominant factor is the amount of dialogue generated. When requirements dictate substantial interaction (student-to-student or facilitator-to-student), transaction volumes increase. This is one of the elements used to determine the number of students that can be served.

The amount of dialogue can be controlled, as suggested in our previous discussion about the learning continuum. The online paradigm lends itself to a number of class-size alternatives. You have seen the learning continuum shown below, but you should review it to help you decide how many students will fit in a class. If you adopt a position toward the Socratic Method end of the continuum, you depend on a higher level of dialogue as a means of learning than if you select a position toward the Independent Study end of the continuum.

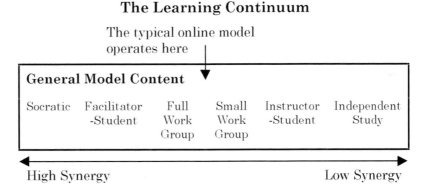

The Learning Continuum

The typical online model operates here

General Model Content					
Socratic	Facilitator -Student	Full Work Group	Small Work Group	Instructor -Student	Independent Study

High Synergy   Low Synergy

Higher levels of dialogue are associated with individual discussion questions and open discussion assignments. Lower dialogue levels result from assignments that focus on individual efforts such as reading and submitting papers.

Why is dialogue level a limitation?

Some types of online classes have generated over 2,400 messages in a six-week period with only 10 students attending. This is 400 messages per week and an average of 40 messages sent by each student. The 40 messages per student represent their individual input including papers, assignments, and comments related to other students' input. Each student is expected to read all messages, which is about 360 per week, excluding his or her own. This represents a major reading and response load for students as well as for the facilitator, who must manage this load while providing appropriate leadership and comments.

Dialogue is a major source of learning in a virtual classroom. Much of the synergy that makes the paradigm attractive comes from these messages. The optimal course design must consider realistically the ability of students and instructors to maintain the expected level of activity. This ultimately limits the number of students who can be accommodated by your course design.

Reconciling the factors

Various factors must be reconciled to reach financial goals. You must maximize the number of students in each class while maintaining an environment that is conducive to learning. Because not all learning situations are alike, you must pursue more than one means of achieving this balance.

As the learning continuum suggests, a number of alternatives can be used in designing online programs. You can select processes that depend on extensive and detailed discussions to achieve learning goals, with synergy being a significant contributor, or you can select an independent study format, in which learning is highly individualized and synergy is less significant. Furthermore, you can select points between the two extremes to meet a specific goal. You can vary the factors to support a class size of 10 to 15 students or a group of 50 or more.

Models

Five basic models describe the flexibility of the virtual classroom, as shown in the following table.

Program Model Summary

Number of Students per Class	Applicable Model	Design Dialogue Levels per Student	
10-15	Interactive	10-12 messages per week	Interactive
15-25	Bounded interactive	5-8 messages per week	Interactive
25-40	Consultative/ interactive	2-5 messages per week	Reduced ineractivity
40-60	Independent/ consultative	Student-facilitator-student only	Non-interactive
Above 60	Special configuration	Varies with design	Special

Interactive

The interactive model is used extensively by institutions across the country. This model uses teaching strategies such as discussion question assignments with answers sent to the VC for comments from other students, experience sharing, group assignments, individual assignments (papers and case studies), and stimulation by the facilitator to achieve the dialogue level necessary for synergy.

This format works well in most classes, and existing curricula can be adapted to it with only minor conversion processes. The instructor's role is very facilitative, and good skills are required for a successful experience.

Bounded interactive

The limited interactive model offers many of the features of the interactive model, but this model limits dialogue to a level that accommodates a larger number of students. This model is used successfully by many institutions. The greatest challenge is in the ability of the curriculum to limit dialogue. If dialogue is not bounded, or limited, the learning experience can be stressful.

The format works well in most classes and can be adapted in large part from an existing curriculum. The conversion process must include consideration of assignments that reduce the level of dialogue while achieving the learning objectives. The instructor's role is very facilitative, and an experienced instructor is required to exercise the appropriate level of control.

Consultative/interactive

This model departs from heavily interactive models in the direction of the independent study end of the learning continuum. Variations of this approach are used by many organizations, especially in hybrid configurations involving supplemental material such as video tapes, face-to-face seminar sessions, and similar teaching techniques. In this model, assignments favor independent efforts while maintaining interactivity in critical subject areas. Group assignments also are involved, and online tools are used to develop these assignments. Secondary materials such as workbooks and handouts are supplied for such programs.

In this model, the facilitator assumes the additional role of consultant to students and must be available on an unlimited basis to answer questions. The facilitator can choose to respond to questions in an online forum accessible to all students or to respond individually to students' questions via a private mailbox.

The facilitator's role is limited in this format and requires less experience than is necessary in the models discussed previously. Content expertise is essential, of course, but highly developed facilitative skills are not as important in this model as in others.

Independent/consultative

This is an independent study model. Online capabilities are used only for communications between students and the facilitator. This model adapts well to existing curricula that focus primarily on individual learning rather than group learning.

Several variations of this model are in use. One involves no direct interaction between students and faculty. The course is designed for independent study, and the materials supplied with the course are designed to be self-supporting. The facilitator's role in this model is that of a subject matter expert, available only through a consulting forum. The forum can be supported by several specialists, if necessary. The number of contacts a student can make is usually limited. This approach works well in certification programs. Final testing can be proctored at a single location or administered online.

A similar model provides flexible start and completion dates for students; otherwise, it is much like the one described above. The VC is used to share questions and answers. Teaching assistants can be assigned to alleviate overloads in certain areas. Students progress incrementally through the curriculum and are tested periodically as a means of advancing from one segment of the curriculum to the next. Tests are not proctored, but a monitored final exam is conducted before certifications are awarded.

Limitations on the number of students who can participate effectively in these classes are related only to the complexity of the subject matter and the types of tools available. Tools such as interactive CD-ROMs, interactive videotapes, Internet research facilities, and others make effective independent study processes possible.

Institutional views toward independent study curricula are varied and must be considered in the design and frequency of use of the Independent/Consultative model.

Special configurations

Special configurations often are used to meet the needs of greater numbers of students. In all cases, the material, locations of participants, and available resources must influence the design.

A feasibility model was recently designed and proposed to a company that wanted to deliver developmental material to large groups of people at multiple locations. Five sites were involved, with between 50 and 300 students at each site. The figure at the end of the section shows the configuration, as well as specific aspects of this approach. Though untested, the elements of this model have been used successfully many times in different combinations.

This model combines technologies. The satellite link is used to send one-way, live, full-motion video and audio signals to the core groups (expandable to provide two-way video and audio). Networked group decision systems can be used as part of breakout sessions or as part of online group activities.

The consulting ring serves as follow-up support for the sessions. The original idea was for a one-day session, with follow-up assignments to be completed after the session. This model can be expanded to support multiple-day sessions or sessions held weekly over a longer time period. The main appeal of this model is the large number of students who can be served, which can justify the cost of the technology.

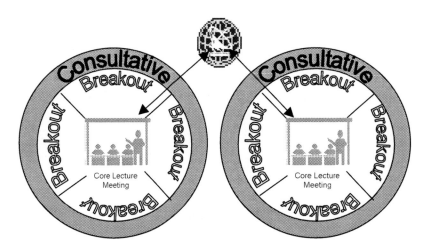

Characteristics of this model include the following:

- The number of core sites is unlimited.

- Each core site can support several hundred participants.

- Breakouts should include about 25 students each. (The number of breakouts is determined by the number of students served at each core site.)

- Breakouts can be serviced by teaching assistants.

- The consulting ring is staffed by a subject matter expert and is conducted online.

In summary

The number of students who can be taught effectively in a class depends on several aspects. This chapter defined the amount of dialogue involved in the process as one key variable. It also explored ways to control dialogue and described models that serve various numbers of students.

You should consider other elements before deciding how many students you can support in a VC. While the interactive model is the most attractive from an academic viewpoint, the financial pressure to operate at the optimal cost level has led to an expanded set of models. Each model has strengths and weaknesses. Each satisfies a different set of criteria present in academic and business environments. Consider your needs and objectives carefully before determining which method to use.

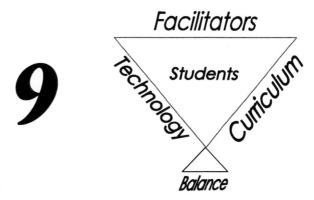

9

Developing and Implementing an Online Program

The key elements required for a successful online learning program have been discussed in previous chapters of this book. It is impractical to suggest that these are the only considerations, but the areas covered thus far cannot be overlooked.

This chapter assumes an understanding of the proper balance of well-designed curricula, well-trained facilitators, and a utility grade technology. This chapter will explore the following elements:

◆ an environment conducive to a successful program

◆ the purpose of a program

◆ the options

- the decision

- the planning

- the costs

The environment

Often the most difficult consideration in developing and implementing an online learning program concerns cultural issues. These issues include faculty members and administrators who will not support the effort, concerns about the effectiveness of online learning, and the institution's ability to assimilate the idea that nontraditional learning models can be a productive and valid means of providing educational opportunities. In overcoming initial cultural issues, the following conditions have proven successful.

- Obtain a champion who is capable of making decisions and is committed to the project.

- Use the services of a professional who is experienced in developing and implementing online programs.

- Provide an environment that is open and supportive of the effort.

- Remove from the process any person who remains uncommitted to the success of the project. (This means every person in the process, not just key people.)

Some environments are not conducive to the successful implementation of an online program. Experience has shown that traditional nonprofit educational institutions can be difficult to work with. In these cases, you may be forced to set up the program development, implementation, and operation within a "skunk works," an operation that is completely separate from the primary institution. This can include securing faculty, administration, and support staff from sources outside the institution. The institution's commitment to the program must be 100%. Members of the institution often inhibit the process, from small misunderstandings to people feeling threatened by a new way of doing things. These people must be removed from the process. The champion decides, based on his or her knowledge of the situation, who will participate and who will not.

> *A champion who is highly skilled and experienced, and who has sufficient influence, can reduce uncertainty and costly mistakes.*

The champion must be a person capable of clearing a path for the process to develop. Without the complete support of a capable and motivated person, the probability of success declines. Typically, vice-presidents, college deans, and executives are designated champions. A person with less influence cannot function effectively in this capacity.

The services of a highly skilled and experienced professional can reduce uncertainty and help prevent the institution from making costly mistakes. The quality of the program depends on thorough consideration of all key elements. To fully understand the various elements that must be balanced, the knowledge of an experienced professional is recommended. Many issues can arise during the development phase of a program, ranging from choosing the best technologies to choosing the kinds of programs that are best suited to the purposes.

Clarity of purpose

Why consider a distance learning program? Clarity of purpose is a key step in the development phase. The exact purpose of such a program is not always obvious. Corporations and other institutions hear of others' successes in offering these programs and want to do the same. Some institutions are scrambling to recapture lost market shares. The purpose of the program should be clearly defined, because this will be the focus that keeps the process on track. Purposes can include:

◆ to increase enrollment

◆ to expand markets

◆ to increase the quality of existing programs

◆ to generate increased revenues with minimal capital

◆ to educate individuals who are unable to access traditional programs

You can use most of the models discussed in this book to increase enrollment numbers. The opportunity for increasing the numbers is derived from issues of convenience, expanded markets, and because of the small cost associated with each additional participant.

Today's society puts a premium on time. Because many adult learners do not have the time to participate in a traditional program, the online alternative becomes very attractive. Online programs easily accommodate persons who cannot commute to a campus for physical, monetary, or geographic reasons. The costs involved in providing a distance learning program will be discussed later in this chapter. The market for distance learning is increasing dramatically as awareness increases.

Markets are expanded by various means using the online model. Entities wanting to offer educational programs can offer a full range, including certification and professional courses, college courses, and personal interest programs. Individuals today are offering personal interest classes online from their homes. Depending on the technology selected, the marketplace can easily be global. Individuals who are separated from the institution by physical barriers become potential customers. Awareness in the market of the effectiveness and convenience of online learning is producing some remarkable data.

The educational world is discovering that many traditional offerings achieve superior results using an online format. Research is beginning to support these claims. The question of whether or not the online learning model is valid and productive exists only in the minds of those unfamiliar with a quality program. Organizations such the Asynchronous Learning Network (ALN), The Sloan Foundation, Colorado State University, and the New Jersey Institute of Technology are producers of primary research in the field.

> *Online programs can have low setup costs and high returns and the ability to penetrate new markets.*

Research also is being conducted in England and European countries. Both the University of Phoenix and Baker College represent the effectiveness of online learning. These programs are accredited and viewed as quality learning experiences in the educational and professional world. At a fraction of the cost of traditional programs to the sponsoring organization, these programs are multiplying at a pace that allows them to be called the fastest growing learning methods in America and possibly, the world.

Online learning programs can be developed and implemented at lower costs than those associated with supporting and maintaining a traditional program. A program can be started with one computer, a modem, a telephone line, and a place to use them. Other types of distance learning programs can cost millions of dollars to implement. What is added value and what is not should be determined in the process of defining the purpose of the program. Net profit margins from established online programs range from 25% to 75%. Many online learning processes feature low setup costs and high returns, and the ability to penetrate new markets is gained in the process.

Asynchronous online models offer anytime/anywhere formats. Because of this, people who would normally be unable to attend a traditional institution can do so from where they are. Some institutions have participants in all 50 states and several foreign countries. Time and distance problems are removed, allowing international participation in many of these programs.

Online programs can do all these things, and a combination of these or other purposes are involved in the decision as to what technology and model is best for the program. Knowing the purpose of providing an online learning program will help guide the remainder of the process.

Various distance learning models are discussed throughout this book. Factors such as the cost of a given option, the number of students who can be effectively accommodated in a class, and the scope and context of the programs also must be considered.

The options

Online technologies today offer a multitude of options. Real-time audio and video, live chat areas, seamless integration of multiple applications, object oriented packages, and simple text-based formats are available. Software providers provide servers, help desks, and delivery of text and software materials to participants. Programs exist that require human interaction on the part of the sponsor once the setup is established.

To determine which model is right for a given situation, ask yourself the following questions:

- What will achieve the purpose?

- What are the economics?

- What is the nature of the course to be offered?

- What options are deemed to be value added by the sponsor?

The fact is, most academic courses are text-based. Because of this, most programs can be offered using a simple asynchronous online model.

Why is video or audio needed in a text-based program? Why is it necessary to bring participants together in a central location? Why are synchronized activities necessary? These services and considerations are needed only in extraordinary circumstances. Highly acclaimed institutions offer over 745 programs, ranging from health care administration to highly advanced computer-based courses to a DBA. Every course uses the same simple text-based asynchronous format. The ever-increasing number of people who participate in the programs attests to the success and effectiveness of the programs.

You must consider the implications of each program requirement. Considering the overall purpose of the program becomes a guiding element. If the purpose of the program is to provide basic educational opportunities to people who otherwise could not access these opportunities, why would you offer a program that requires a high-end computer system and a superior level of computer knowledge to participate?

Understanding the capabilities of the market you are seeking is critical. If a program requires that all systems have multimedia capabilities, those who do not have these capabilities cannot

Until the capability of the market has increased, change must remain an evolving process.

participate. This raises the question of what the lowest common denominator (LCD) should be in a program, in terms of technology. If a course in computer networking is offered, the LCD will probably be a system that has multimedia capabilities. Running demonstrations and labs on a CD-ROM demands that the system has a CD-ROM drive.

The LCD also affects curriculum development. If a program is developed with a specified system requirement of a 486SX processor with a 540MB hard disk and 8MB of RAM, every course in that program is limited to that level. Once a program is instituted (especially a program that takes several years to complete), changing technologies can cause difficulties. It is a long-term process at best. Selection criteria for a technology package should include the capacity to be upgraded over time. Introducing new versions of software and increasing system requirements (as the typical user system capability increases) is one way to build capabilities over time. The curriculum and tools used in the learning process cannot be changed until all participants in the process can meet the minimum system requirements.

You can require that the minimum system have Microsoft Windows 95 with a 2GB hard disk and 32MB of RAM, but much of the market is still using systems with DOS capabilities and little hard disk capacity or RAM. As mentioned earlier in the book, 1000 of 1400 participants in one of the nation's leading distance educational programs are operating with DOS on low end systems.

In this case, a significant portion of the institution's market would be lost by changing the system requirements. Until the norm in the market has increased in capability, change must be an evolving process. In many cases, it is a matter of what customers can afford. It is important to recognize that any additional requirement can affect existing and potential markets. Know your market.

In developing the distance learning program, we have given consideration to the following:

◆ the purpose of the program

◆ the institution's resource capabilities

◆ the environment needed to conduct the development

◆ the learning model used

◆ the technology used

◆ the participants' ability to participate and the expectations of participants

Consideration must be given to curricula, facilitators, support and service mechanisms, and the cost options of various programs. If the entity offering a program has defined its purposes and explored the technological options in relation to system requirements and how these requirements will affect participation, some understanding of the kinds of courses to be offered will either be implied or identified specifically.

The curriculum, as discussed in Chapter 5, must be either converted or developed. In either case, a content expert and a trained facilitator will be needed to do the job properly. Companies sell curricula designed to be used for distance learning programs. To date, the information gathered indicates that these companies primarily cater to learning models that use videotapes and workbooks. The time required to develop or convert a curriculum depends on the nature of the material and the ability of the developers. A facilitator who has experience in using the learning model and technology can provide valuable information as to which tools are effective, how the curriculum can be converted to meet the learning objectives, and can provide valuable input to the subject matter expert.

Expectations of facilitators have been discussed throughout the book. The need for highly trained and experienced facilitators is critical to the success of the program. Many institutions developing distance learning courses for the first time may find that going outside the institution is required to staff

> *Consideration must be given to curricula, facilitators, support and service mechanisms, and the cost options of various programs.*

the program. Good programs exist for training facilitators. If the trained facilitator lacks experience, a mentorship is suggested, to continue until the facilitator is comfortable with the process. The right balance must be maintained between the facilitator and the curriculum.

Customer service is another aspect discussed earlier in this book, which cannot be overlooked. All participants in the program, including students, facilitators, technical support staff, and customer service staff should be supported in a timely and professional manner. The scope and depth of the required support structure will be determined by the technology used and the size of the program. The level of service is not an option; the system must be responsive and easy to access.

Online program planning

Every successful event gives evidence of prior careful, comprehensive planning strategies. Online program planning is critical to developing a successful online program. Socrates$^©$ DLTG uses a two-phase, six element planning approach called Online Program Planning$^©$. By addressing each of the six elements within the two phases, an organization or institution betters its chances of bringing a successful, sustainable online program into existence.

Phase One of Online Program Planning includes the following elements:

1. Overview of online concepts

2. Define key client program elements

3. Identify team resource requirements

Phase Two of Online Program Planning includes the following elements:

4. Develop detailed project plans

5. Pilot option

6. Launch production program

Online Education

Online Program Planning©

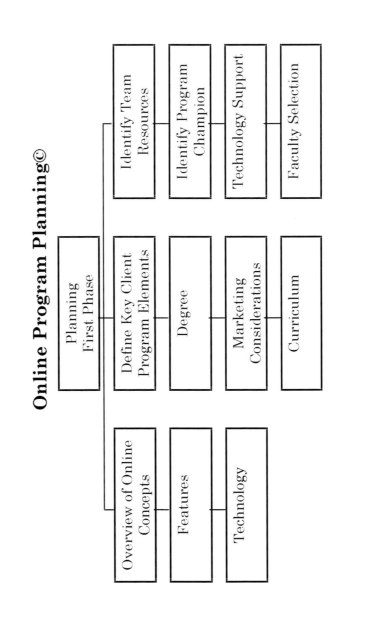

Online Program Planning©

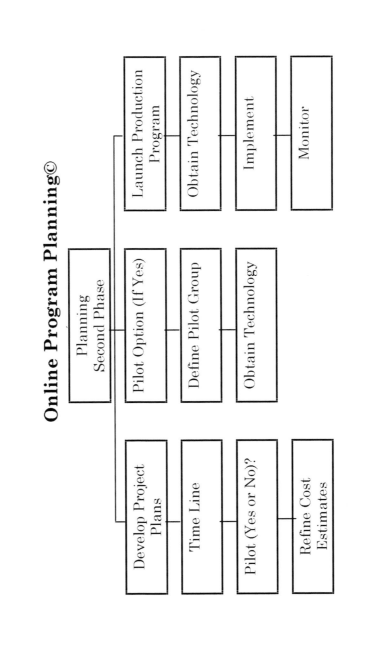

Costs

The issues involved in various online programs have been explored in sufficient depth in this book to create awareness. Costs are associated with operating a distance learning program. In looking at the costs of implementing, operating, and maintaining a program, the following scenario is designed to offer some ideas.

A major university has decided to develop, implement, and operate an asynchronous online learning program, using Convene as the primary technology package. In addition, costing has been provided for an Internet-based technology. Embanet is the option selected.

Convene has been selected as the primary provider of the asynchronous online program. Two options exist in using Convene. Convene servers and infrastructure can be used, or the institution can bring the operation in-house. This costing structure will consider only the use of Convene servers. Costs of bringing the operation in-house depend on available resources and resources that must be obtained to meet the demands of the proposed program.

Developmental costs

Consulting costs

Consulting fees for program development typically run $1000 per day plus $500 per day for associated expenses for onsite time, $150 per hour for telephone consulting support. The total estimated cost for a typical University program (asynchronous online) will run $13,000. This will take the customer from initial contact through a successful pilot program.

Administration

Administration is typically integrated into the existing capacity of the organization. Initially the Administration function is estimated to require 30 payroll days at a cost of $150 per day per person; probably two people working half time. This will vary between organizations. Total for initial development and set up $4,500.

(In many cases the sponsoring organization has the excess capacity within the organization to absorb the costs of payroll and enrollment activities associated with the program in the future, the capacity of the organization will dictate additional costs in this area).

Developmental Cost Model

Developmental Costs	Initial Development
Consulting fees	Approximately $13,000
Administration	Approximately $4,500
Curriculum conversion	Averages $500 per conversion
Setup costs technology	Varies between $0 and $1,000
Facilitator costs	$1,500 per course
Expense to students	Computer
Software expense to students	Varies between $0 and $30 per student

Curriculum conversion and development

Costs associated with curriculum conversion and development will range from $500 dollars for a conversion to $2,000 for a full-blown development. The costs here will vary by region, by complexity of content, and by resources available. The initial figure we used here is $2,000 dollars. As the organization gains experience with the processes, the tools, and the technology the costs will come down.

Initial Advertising and marketing costs typically integrated into existing marketing/advertising budgets. These expenses will vary dramatically between public institutions, private institutions, and corporations. $5,000 dollars is an initial number typically used in public institutions.

Getting a program from the initial discussion to the completion of an initial pilot program will run approximately $20,500.

In summary

The costs of developing, implementing, and operating a distance learning program vary among institutions. Developing a distance learning program requires that the institution obtain experienced and professional help. The purpose of the program is the basis for building the program. The overall purpose can include multiple goals; because of this, the choice of technologies can become complex. The facilitator, the curriculum, the technology and the support structures must all be considered in developing the program. What is the optimal LCD for the required technology? Is streaming video a value added part of a learning program? Much of this is subjective and can be answered only through program development and implementation. Typically, given the help of a professional, the time required to develop and implement an asynchronous online program is about 90 days.

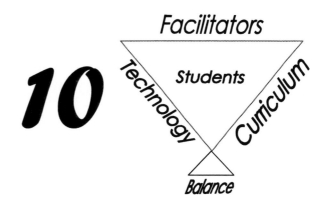

Does Online Have a Role in My Institution or Business?

Introduction

We have discussed online education from several different perspectives in the previous chapters with pros and cons along the way. Now is the time to ask: Is an online program for my institution or business? Do enough of the concepts offered fit together in a way that we could expect a payoff if we are to implement a program?

This chapter will try to answer these questions, or at a minimum, provide a framework for you to answer this question for your organization.

Where will online work?

This question is being answered every day by organizations that are seeking solutions to their training or educational problems. And the simple answer is anywhere that a strong enough need exists to gain support for the concept. In most areas, institutions that are considering online as a solution or partial solution to their educational problems, limitations must be overcome before any online program can be successful. Thus, the reference to "...enough need exists to gain support for the concept."

For example, let's consider a situation where a need has been defined to improve the grammar skills of a diverse group of people in a geographically disbursed area with a radius of 50 miles from the institution considering the program offering. When the demographics of this "community" is reviewed, one notices that the majority of the population involved works across three shifts in facilities scattered around the 50-mile radius. Most are family people and cannot easily allocate the time necessary to travel to the institution. Classes of 15 to 20 people might be possible, but workweeks are scattered across all seven days of the week and shift schedules vary. This will make it difficult to find one time to meet that would be achievable for everyone.

Certainly, the on-ground class alternative should be considered first since this is the normal mode of operation for the institution and would require little in terms of change, incremental resources, or new technologies. However, one very significant problem identified in the above scenario is that it is difficult to accommodate the on-ground format—the time students are available to attend classes. Since they work across three shifts, it will be difficult, if not impossible, to define a time where you could conveniently bring enough students together to form a class. You likely would be unsuccessful in serving this need with the traditional delivery system. Elements such as travel time are significant, but it is possible that the potential students could arrange solutions to this.

This appears to be an opportunity for the online alternative. The downside includes the need to develop, implement, and help students and faculty perform in this new delivery method. The upside includes:

1. a solution that may offer the opportunity for attendance for a greater number of people in need

2. the possibility of using the resources for expanding the options for supplying to the needs of others in the service area

3. consideration of the trends in educational delivery, which suggests many innovative methods are needed to meet the diverse needs of most student coverage areas

To determine whether an online delivery is appropriate, we might consider the following factors:

1. Are the potential students sufficiently computer literate for an online program?

2. Could the usual resistance to technology be overcome with this group?

3. Do the perspective students have ready access to home computers?

4. Can the subject we are going to offer be presented in an online format?

5. Are cost-effective communications facilities available to potential students?

6. Can such a program be successfully implemented within the cultural boundaries of the institution, or is the institution willing to adapt?

These questions address a number of possible roadblocks, but none of these items are fatal to a program if the sponsoring institution and individuals are sufficiently driven by the needs to resolve these areas of concern.

For example, if computer literacy is a problem, and you are willing to provide focused training to assure that students are properly trained to be successful in an online computer-based educational process, you can provide for this need in a very short time. (One to three weeks of instruction are enough.) Resistance to technology is a significant challenge, but programs to reduce this concern exist, and it is entirely possible to bring this factor into control.

If not all of the potential students have computers, how can you address this need? You might make computer laboratories available for use by those who are close to the base institution. If the need is in a financially challenged area of the city, you may want to ask for community support for the project and fund either a loan service or a giving program. Also, you may be able to have companies donate computers that are outdated for their use but that might be good for educational programs.

A program such as that suggested in the preceding scenario is a good candidate for online delivery, and there are examples available in the educational arena for review. If your organization does not have the skills to develop courseware and procedures for an online experience, you can subcontract resources that are capable of performing this task until you develop such resources in your organization. In some cases, you may find another institution willing to share their materials with you.

The cultural boundaries issue may well be the most difficult challenge in the list. If the organization is resistant to change and to technological solutions to educational challenges, implementation may become a major issue. Faculty resistance is of particular concern as the time to overcome such concerns can be extensive. The "skunk works" approach may be an alternative. This is discussed elsewhere in this book.

There is the possibility that the subject area you are considering is not totally a candidate for online delivery. There may be segments that just don't lend themselves to online presentation. You may want to consider a hybrid approach to meeting this need. Hybrids will be discussed in greater detail at a later point in this book.

If telephone costs become an issue for the population you are serving, you can provide 1-800 (free) phone access to the system you are using. Or, you can select a technology that minimizes this concern in the mind of the students.

We could add to this list and find many additional limitations that will create a challenge in ANY implementation plan, online or on-ground. However, if we need to or want to minimize these limitations, we could do that with appropriate funding and resource availability.

In the preceding scenario, depending on the criticality of the need for grammar skill improvements, you may want to use the online approach as a solution to the problem of accessibility. If you are an educational institution and businesses in the community are withholding support of your programs unless you help solve the problems that workers bring to the workplace from their former educational processes, you may find providing these accommodations necessary. This may be deemed

Chapter 10 – Does Online Have a Role in My Institution or Business?

149

worthwhile to position you positively in your relationships with the community and business leaders.

On the other hand, if you are a business and the costs of such a project are beyond company means, you may be unwilling to add the burden of administering such a program if it involves the limitations noted in the scenario. You recognize the costs as a direct drop to the bottom line, which would potentially impact your marketplace viability. So you put pressure on the local educational resources to provide solutions to the grammar shortfall.

As noted, very few subject areas could not be satisfied, at least in part, by an online program. This is applicable in both the academic areas as well as the area of industry-offered training. The organization considering using online as a solution must either have resources who are experienced with online learning or seek assistance in developing, planning, and implementing their program. A faulty implementation may increase resistance to moving the program forward; doing it right the first time is very important.

When considering whether a course can be implemented online, it is helpful to develop a profile of the learning objectives and the tools and methods available in the online format to meet these needs. Usually short lectures, carefully crafted discussion questions, and readings form the core tools for presenting materials. But if your program requires laboratories, special tools, or special materials (like artwork for an art appreciation class), you need to consider how you might provide for these needs. For example,

Develop a profile of the learning objectives and the tools and methods available in the online format to meet these needs.

laboratories can be simulated with specially designed interactive CD-ROMs. Special tools might include survey instruments, statistical programs, or special software that can be satisfied by packaging ancillaries or providing shared access to applications such as statistical programs. Special materials may be provided as mail-outs with the registration materials, supplemental CD-ROMs, access to special online library sources, and a number of other alternatives. In extreme cases, this may be where you identify the need for supplemental on-ground meetings to cover certain aspects of an assignment. This is rare, but may be required. At times, these contact needs can be served by teleconferences, videoconferences, or chat connections.

Areas where online programs may not be applicable

To this point, we have implied that there is a solution to any need and online is universally applicable; however, this is not true. Areas exist where online programs simply are not the best way to do the job, and we need to recognize this. We need to be cautious in discarding an opportunity without careful consideration, because some of the solutions are not obvious and will require innovative efforts.

Let us assume we are a medical school considering offering programs that lead to becoming a doctor. We are looking at three areas that we may want to offer in an online format: pharmacology, anatomy, and fundamentals of surgery.

Several schools offer or are considering offering pharmacology courses, particularly post-graduate courses to upgrade skills. With a combination of course design factors that provide an individual with easy access to the professor

Chapter 10 – Does Online Have a Role in My Institution or Business?

151

for support; workbook-type materials for the student to follow in self-study mode; interactive CD-ROMs for identification, laboratory, and other kinds of visually related needs; and testing processes that assure learning objectives are accomplished. Some schools retain a residency requirement somewhere in the program that must be fulfilled, but most of the course is offered online.

Anatomy is another course that readily adapts to online presentation. Computer-based simulations and visual materials are readily available to support this program. We will leave the details for later, but this is a course that could be easily adapted to an online/independent study format.

Fundamentals of surgery present some interesting problems. There are many components of this program that could be presented online or as a supplement on groundwork,

> *There are areas where online education is not the best solution.*

but some areas definitely do not lend themselves to online learning. Tools are being developed that may make it possible to simulate surgical procedures through virtual reality tactile programs. These programs are used in many on-ground programs and as they are perfected, it is technically possible to present them online. In this case, there may be a case for restructuring the course to separate the parts of the program that can be adapted to online. This could use ancillaries such as videotapes, CD-ROMs, closed-circuit TV programming, and other tools. The remaining parts of the program will need to be provided for in the traditional ways until proven tactile processes can be used to simulate surgery. Even then, hands-on mentorships and practicuums will be required to complete the work.

This example is extreme, but it serves to dramatically demonstrate how a program could be unbundled and the element requirements be provided for in multiple ways, including online components.

Hybrid models

As you will note in the preceding scenarios, many times the need is not fully satisfied by a simple "convert the current curriculum to online" approach. Courses with high visual content, graphics requirements, physical intervention needs, and face-to-face components do not automatically convert to online. Special requirements need special actions. In first assessing the viability of an online program, it would be easy to eliminate all but the most fundamental programs, based on needs that are not obviously compatible with online technologies. Yet, after segmenting the elements of the program into categories such as "directly convertible," "convertible with limitations," and "no apparent online way to achieve," the planners will see that most of the program is adaptable with a relatively minor effort. Even in the "no apparent online way to achieve" category, most needs can be met with available or easily produced tools.

Once programs have been divided into these categories, some elements may be left that cannot be directly satisfied or modified. These may need to be serviced by a hybrid system.

In the context of an online program, a hybrid system can be defined as:

Chapter 10 – Does Online Have a Role in My Institution or Business?

153

The combining of the typical online
processes with other processes as necessary
to deliver the planned learning outcomes for
the course.

A hybrid often combines online sessions and on-ground
components. The construct can focus on the program being
online with supplementary on-ground work. Or, the focus
can be on ground, with supplementary online portions.
Many existing hybrids offer a portion of the course or
program online and other
portions in residence at the
sponsoring institution. This
is attractive to more
traditional institutions that
have difficulty accepting a
model that might result in
the student graduate not
ever visiting the degree-
granting institution.

> *An infinite number
> of possibilities for
> packaging learning
> modules can be
> used to meet the
> needs of groups in
> convenient ways.*

Other variations can be considered, such as satellite one- or
two-way video broadcasts to central locations in multiple
cities, where students can gather and interact with the
facilitator. The work done in these sessions can be
supplemented by online work. In some cases, this model is
used as a way to bring noted speakers in a particular
subject area to a large but diversified group of students.
Audio teleconferencing is another possible supplementary
tool for use in hybrids. An infinite number of possibilities
for packaging learning modules can be used to meet the
needs of groups in convenient ways.

A caution regarding hybrid systems: Generally, while these
adaptations add functionality, they also add cost and
inconvenience to a program. In the case of interactive
satellite programs, for example, you may add several

thousand dollars in costs and significant inconveniences to a very diversified student audience. If interactive satellites are essential to meeting the program objectives, this technology should be included. But the alternative of distributing videotapes of the speaker, with programmed materials to cover the content of the subject area, might be a more economical and less stressful alternative.

In summary

The online paradigm is very adaptable and can be used as a means of delivering a wide range of programs in academic or business institutions. As technology advances, there are more and more ways to adapt to the special needs of groups and courses with complex content. At this time, one means of overcoming limitations to the fundamental online model is through hybrid adaptations.

To a large extent, the adaptability of educational programs to online delivery is limited only by the flexibility that the organization is willing to apply in overcoming roadblocks. Often, these roadblocks are simply challenges that need to be studied and solved within the framework of the online paradigm. This requires the support of people who are familiar with online concepts; this is often beyond the knowledge base of those currently in the institution. This need may need to be fulfilled by sharing information and experiences with similar institutions that have successful programs or by employing consultants who are experienced in developing and implementing online programs.

Chapter 10 – Does Online Have a Role in My Institution or Business?

155

11

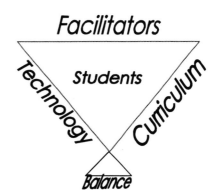

Marketing Online Programs

Introduction

There are unique challenges in marketing online courses. The challenges are particularly critical for the institution that is making an initial offering of online programs. While many of the processes used in marketing the on-ground courses will apply later in the program, initially, the institution will likely be required to employ unique strategies to establish their presence in the online markets. Once an institution is established as an online course provider, normal marketing strategies supplemented by focused programs, will support growth and sustained performance.

It is important to recognize that while many institutions have some method for offering DISTANCE EDUCATION programs, we are differentiating online programs as being a special category of distance learning requiring additional considerations.

This chapter will provide a number of strategies for marketing programs at the onset and on a continuing basis.

Where are online students?

At this time, most institutional online recruiting strategies focus on reaching students that are not now attending colleges because of the limitations of family, workplace, physical proximity to classrooms, physical personal limitations, or any of several other reasons for not being able to attend the normal classroom offerings. Such institutions do not want to see a reduction in their ongoing enrollments as a result of adding online programs - they expect the online enrollment to be incremental to the existing programs. This is rapidly changing for institutions that have established online programs - they are finding it useful to offer both formats. The marketing strategies discussed in this chapter are mainly focused on incremental recruiting, although many of the processes could also be used for in-house recruiting.

An additional parameter that needs consideration in determining our audience and strategies for recruiting is geographical. Some programs may be limited to an area set by the state or county that is funding the institution. Other institutions want to grow their student body be recruiting nationally or even internationally.

Within these parameters, students will most likely come from one or more of the following areas:

1. From the outlying areas in proximity to the offering institution. These students are physically within range of the institution but the travel time and conflicts with other schedules may discourage participation in on-ground classes.

2. Factories and businesses within range of the offering institution that may employ potential students that would have schedule conflicts prohibiting or complicating on-ground classroom attendance.

3. Other institutions or departments that could benefit from unique courses offered by your institution. Normally these students would need to have classes available during non-working times. They may also be geographically disbursed (but intrastate).

4. Alumni of the institution. Normally these people are highly involved and can only consider classes that are conveniently offered.

5. Trade associations.

6. Military bases.

7. Organizations representing the physically challenged.

8. People who are on summer vacations from educational institutions and have time for special classes.

9. Students resulting from alliances between your institution and another institution or business. This is particularly useful in international projects.

10. Students from specialized industries such as Health Care, Information Systems, Education, Real Estate, etc. where certificate programs can be developed and delivered.

11. From a wider geographical area than their immediate boundaries (interstate, nationally or internationally).

12. From existing students on a very controlled basis. For example, prerequisite courses can be offered to students of the institution online and this can SUPPORT institutional objectives rather than compete with them. Courses that cannot be offered conveniently on-ground are candidates for offering online.

This list is unlimited as the concept of online is offered to groups and the advantages to them are explored. This often requires someone going to these institutions or organizations and making presentations in an effort to "educate" the potential students.

Timing considerations

Because the processes for marketing and recruiting for online programs have unique components, timing becomes a challenge - particularly for the initial offerings of classes. Because the organization is not familiar with online processes, significant time is required to bring the support functions up to speed on the marketing requirements for the program. Then marketing materials must be prepared and distributed prior to students enrolling. Usually a period of six to nine months prior to the initial class is required for a full-scale marketing effort to be in place.

The initial offering—a special case

With these elements in mind, initial recruiting will usually end up as a special circumstance and will generally not come directly from the institutional marketing resources. While the marketing function may well participate in the activities, the actual class will often be recruited by special efforts initiated by Program Management, Faculty, and selected administrators. This is happening while the marketing function is developing their strategies and materials for the longer-term support of the program.

In the following paragraphs, the unique nature of the initial offering is considered apart from the mainstream marketing and recruiting efforts. The special circumstances involved are considered and strategies are offered for this event. Then, more generalized marketing and recruiting strategies are discussed.

Institutions that are just beginning programs in the online market must deal with several constraints including:

1. The institution has no name recognition in the online markets - they may be established general education or distance learning areas but not in the online markets.

2. There are not yet students to pass along information regarding the program to other possible candidate.

3. The marketing functions within the institution have little or no experiences in preparing materials, selecting target segments, or identifying marketing possibilities for offering online programs.

4. The marketing efforts are often delayed until late in the program and many times the initial class enrollments cannot depend on the Marketing function to support student-recruiting efforts for the first classes.

Suggested strategies for the initial offering

There are very limited alternatives for subscribing the first group to attend an online class. The following lists the most accessible sources for short-term recruiting and possible strategies for this to take place.

1. Recruit from existing students on a very controlled basis. For example, prerequisite courses can be offered to students of the institution online and this can SUPPORT institutional objectives rather than compete with them. Courses that cannot for some reason be offered conveniently on-ground are candidates for offering online.

    Strategy: Offer the first course series as a Certificate program. Identify 10-15 students for each class to be conducted from related groups within the institution that would have reason to take the certificate program. Offer them the program at a discounted rate in recognition of the pilot nature of he program.

2. Contact people who are on summer vacations from educational institutions and have time for special classes.

    Strategy: Contact key people in other institutions in the area you serve. Use your informal networks where appropriate. Provide a briefing package for their use in contacting individuals in their institutions that would benefit from the program. You can choose to offer discounts or not - depending on your anticipated results.

3. Contact other institutions or departments that could benefit from unique courses offered by your institution. Normally these students would need to have classes

available during non-working times. They may also be geographically disbursed (but intrastate).

Use the same strategies employed in one and two above.

4. Recruit alumni of the institution. Normally these people are highly involved and can only consider classes that are conveniently offered.

Strategy: Make a contact through the alumni association and offer the classes with an alumni discount of 25%. Seek only alumni that are currently working in areas that would benefit from the certificate work.

Also, this would be a good area to test out direct mailing materials on a limited and focused basis. The relatively short timing could be accommodated by providing online registration backed up by on-ground registration support.

Strategies for reaching students— after the initial offering

The following table represents several strategies for reaching potential students with a link to the areas in which such students can be found. The strategies are general in nature and could probably be applied across more than is defined below.

Note that most of these strategies will take some time to implement and may not be useful to the institution's initial offering due to the timing.

Recruiting Strategies

STRATEGY	Applies to items listed in "Where are online students?"
Catalogs (the major institutional catalog)	1
Catalog (special distribution for online only)	2-12
Selected media advertising (longer term)	All
Selected media (short term - newspaper, etc.)	8, 10
Direct mailing (general)	All
Direct mailing (focused groups)	2, 12
Professional solicitation (personal basis)	All
Direct solicitation from classes or chairs	8, 12
Contact with institutional training functions	2, 3, 5, 6, 8, 10
Postings on bulleting boards (within the institution)	8, 12
Presentations to trade associations	5
Presentations to conferences	All
Publication by the institutions staff	All
Web pages	All

In summary

When a program is planned, ultimately someone will ask the question "Who is our audience?" This will often be someone who will be trying to reach students for recruiting purposes. And - this ultimately will lead to the marketing arm of the institution.

This chapter just touches on the complex subject of marketing and is intended to provide a stating point for those responsible for online programs. Getting started is the main challenge - after a program is underway, there are a number of tools that are suitable for maintaining growth.

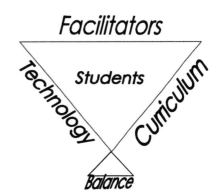

12

Expectations of the Elements in an Online Learning Process

This chapter summarizes the basic concepts of distance learning programs and, in particular, the online learning process. By focusing on expectations, it is possible to derive the elements necessary for a successful program.

Reasonable expectations of an online program take many forms. The information presented in this chapter is what Socrates© Distance Learning Technologies Group considers the optimal characteristics and qualities to look for in the elements of a successful online program.

A basic understanding of what to expect from facilitators, curricula, technologies, students, and customer service elements will enhance your overall understanding of a quality online program.

The facilitator

In order to develop and maintain an online program that is effective and smooth and will achieve the learning objectives, the facilitator must play a vital role. While most seasoned instructors within the traditional realm will easily adapt to the online model, many will not. The need for online faculty training often is underestimated. The facilitator in an online environment must possess a unique set of qualities to perform effectively. The following list contains a set of reasonable expectations of the characteristics, capabilities, and personal attributes of those who can successfully facilitate online distance learning programs.

1. Facilitators are considered to be clinical, that is, they are broadly experienced and have a solid business-related background.

    This is a real-world learning model, and it requires facilitators who know what the real world is about. Experience is a good teacher and builds a level of understanding of issues that far surpasses any other kind of learning. Online facilitators must be experienced in real-world business and have a solid grasp of the subjects they teach. Current knowledge of practices within the subject matter is a key part of providing usable education.

2. The personality of a facilitator should reflect openness, sensitivity, concern, flexibility, and sincerity.

Online students are as busy or busier than anyone else in today's hurried world. Students are the customers and must be treated as such. The characteristics mentioned above are not optional; they are essential.

3. Facilitators must communicate well in writing.

    Face-to-face contact is absent from the online learning process. Verbal communication is replaced by electronic communication through the keyboard. This communication is intense and demanding. The facilitator must be comfortable communicating in writing, because that is the basis of the process.

4. Facilitators should believe in the advantage of facilitated learning over traditional learning models.

    A teacher who feels that true learning can occur only through traditional means of educating is not a good candidate for an online facilitator's position. The on-ground classroom experience cannot be duplicated in the online paradigm.

5. Facilitators should value critical thinking in the learning process.

    The online learning process is designed to facilitate the assimilation of theory into both conceptual and applied knowledge. Students expect to receive knowledge and abilities they can use in the workplace. This requires the ability to think critically.

6. Facilitators must have the appropriate credentials to teach the subject matter.

Universities and corporations are full of people who have the knowledge to teach a given subject matter. A college degree and experience in traditional learning models is not enough to ensure success in an online paradigm. Faculty members must be trained and/or experienced in the particular learning model used as well as in the subject matter.

7. Facilitators should be experienced and well trained in online learning programs.

Faculty members should be certified through an approved Socrates© DLTG program. Experience with the tools used in facilitating online programs, appropriate ways of communicating with students online, controlling the flow of work in the VC, and knowing how to prepare a course are just a few of the expectations placed on a facilitator.

What should students in an online learning experience expect from a facilitator? The following is a list of reasonable expectations.

◆ Students can expect the facilitator to create a learning environment in which life, work, and educational experiences are key elements in the learning process.

◆ A facilitator should present the curriculum in a manner that allows students to easily translate theory into applied knowledge.

◆ Students must be given the proper tools to transcribe theory into practice.

◆ Every student should be given every opportunity to improve throughout the learning experience.

- Reasonable accommodations should be made for students' needs and desires.

- A facilitator should solicit feedback from students and listen to what they say throughout the process.

- A facilitator must always be concerned about students' success.

- Students should expect little or no lecturing; lecturing is the least productive method of teaching.

- Students should not be subjected to tests requiring memorization. Case analyses are more appropriate.

- Students should always be treated politely and with respect.

- A facilitator should be online every day; a facilitator must be online at least five of seven days.

This list is not complete, but it provides guidelines for what students can expect of a facilitator and what a good facilitator should offer students. In the online paradigm, a quality facilitator can make a great deal of difference in attaining learning objectives.

Facilitators must possess a unique set of qualities and play a vital role in an online program.

The student

Like facilitators, online students must possess unique qualities. Online students today are primarily working people trying to create better professional opportunities for themselves. This is changing, however, as more and more people, young and old, become familiar with online programs. Traditional schools will never vanish, but the virtual classroom is a significant part of today's educational community. Corporations use online models to train technical professionals, while private and public universities are redefining the world as their market, which is rapidly expanding. Online students should possess the following qualities:

◆ be open-minded about sharing life, work, and educational experiences as part of the learning process

Introverts as well as extroverts find that the online process requires them to share their experiences. The forum for communication eliminates visual barriers that hinder some individuals in expressing themselves. In addition, students are given time to consider their answers before responding. It is an open and friendly environment.

◆ be able to communicate in writing

Students, as much as anyone else in the process, must be comfortable expressing themselves in writing.

◆ be self-motivated

With freedom and flexibility comes responsibility; the online process requires real commitment and discipline to keep up with the flow of learning.

◆ be able to commit four to six hours a week per course

Online learning is no easier than learning in traditional educational processes, in fact, many students say it requires more time and commitment.

◆ be able to meet the minimum technological requirements of the program

Requirements for online are no less than those for any other quality educational program.

◆ be able to accept critical thinking and decision making as part of the learning process

The learning process requires that students make decisions based on facts as well as experience: assimilating information and executing the right decisions requires critical thought; case analysis does this very effectively.

◆ be able to access a computer, a telephone line, and a modem

The communication medium consists of these three items. Students must have access to the necessary equipment.

◆ feel that high quality learning can take place outside a traditional classroom

If students feel that a traditional classroom is needed in order to learn anything, they might be more comfortable in a traditional classroom; online is not for everyone.

◆ be able to think ideas through before responding

Meaningful and quality input in the VC is an essential part of the learning process. Time is allotted in the process for careful consideration of responses. Testing and challenging ideas is encouraged. Students are not always right, but they should always be prepared for a challenge.

Students who would rather be on traditional campuses attending traditional classrooms are probably not going to be happy online. Though the level of social contact can be very high in the VC, given that many barriers come down online, it is not like living in a dorm on a campus. Online students can be expected to:

- participate in the VC five of seven days a week
- work with others in completing projects
- use the technology properly
- meet minimum standards set forth by the institution
- complete assignments on time
- enjoy communicating in writing

The online learning process is normally accelerated and requires commitment on the students' part. Keeping up with the class and completing all work on time is vital. Once a student gets behind, it is almost impossible to catch up. Students must want to participate and must want the experience.

> *Students must possess unique qualities and be committed to the online learning process.*

The curriculum

The curriculum is an easily overlooked element in the development of an online program. Many attempts are made to duplicate traditional on-ground curricula in the online paradigm; it does not work. Curricula adapted to an online environment must provide the following:

> *A well designed online curriculum leads to a learning process that is second to none.*

- ◆ achievable learning outcomes

- ◆ a learning process that incorporates the life, work, and educational experiences of students and facilitator

- ◆ a continual stream of dialogue concerning the subject matter

- ◆ an association between the concepts learned and practical workplace applications

- ◆ case analyses, exercises, and other application-oriented materials to be used in the VC to help students put theory into practice

- ◆ ample time for activities and applications and minimal lecturing

- ◆ minimal memorization, which must be functional.

  Students should not be required to memorize anything they cannot use in their job setting.

- a workable relationship between the technology, the facilitator, and the students

- group and team activities that are integral to the learning model

A well designed online curriculum leads to a learning process that is second to none. An appropriate curriculum and a well-prepared facilitator are not enough, however. The technology also must support the needs of the users.

> *The technology and customer service systems must provide reliable service.*

The technology

Many distance learning technologies exist. The online model is excellent for providing distance learning. Expectations of the technology should include the following:

- a system that is understandable and user-friendly

- reliable connections to the host

- a format that supports the learning objectives

- quick and easy access to technical support

- technology that is affordable to the institution and to students

- technology that is backed by a company that will provide modifications to the software as new needs arise

- consistent software

The expectations of technology listed are reasonable and necessary to maintaining a functional online program.

Customer service

Customers involved with online learning enjoy the process, but only when it works. Customer service is a vital aspect of online learning. Programs can be developed that are virtually trouble-free, but people new to the system will need help at times. Facilitators can resolve some issues, technology providers can resolve some, and a help desk can resolve some. But students and instructors alike must know where to turn for help. Though this sounds easy, experience shows that customer service demands particular attention. These programs are expected to work and produce results; anything less is unacceptable.

In summary

Here is a summary of the key aspects of a successful online program:

- Faculty - the right person, well trained and experienced
- Curriculum - properly generated or converted, matched to the process
- Student - the right person, properly motivated and prepared
- Technology - the right package to meet the needs
- Customer Service - easily accessed and effective

If you can achieve these five goals, you are off to an exciting and productive future in online education.

13

Facilitators

Technology

Students

Curriculum

Balance

The Future

Introduction

> Universities won't survive. The future is
> outside the traditional campus, outside the
> traditional classroom. Distance learning is
> coming on fast.

These words of Peter Drucker set the stage for a discussion
of the future of online education. Only in the past three to
five years have we seen references to distance learning, and
specifically online learning, coming from thought leaders in
business and education. Until this time, these programs
were more like underground movements, operated by
lesser-known institutions that prided themselves in being
on the leading edge of educational technology. In the next
five to ten years, the following trends listed will begin to
materialize:

- Most educational institutions in the U.S. and to some extent worldwide will adopt online education as a major method of delivering curricula to students.

- The majority of users of online concepts today are in the adult educational areas. Within the next few years, this will extend to high schools, grade schools, and home education programs.

- Corporate education will be a major user of online educational concepts to deliver training, management development, and other educational needs to their employees worldwide.

- Delivery technologies will develop in several areas, including interactive television, cable, and telephone options from the home; special Internet-like services for high quality educational experiences in video, interactive audio, and multi-media offerings; and satellite center program delivery will become an affordable reality for the masses.

- Distributed education will become a viable option and will offer opportunities to students to build a custom degree program to be taken online from multiple, worldwide educational sources. This will make available the best of the best.

- The need to redevelop the workforce will become a major national priority, and online educational concepts will play a major role in meeting this need.

- Programs will need to consider the international educational environment in order to be viable and to take advantage of the resources available in the worldwide arena.

These trends will develop because online technologies and concepts fit the needs of an evolving population. The workforce is time-constrained, yet must be further educated to survive in the even faster-paced workplace of tomorrow. The ability to receive educational materials wherever you are is a very appealing alternative to traveling to a classroom regularly to obtain the materials.

The educational challenge of the next century

Change has been with us since the beginning of time, but the rate of change has been relatively slow, providing time to adapt and assimilate new information. Over the past 25 years, the rate of change has dramatically accelerated and challenges many of the systems that have worked for us in the past. Educational sources predict that graduates will experience five to seven complete career changes during their working lifetimes. This means that while the educational systems of today prepare people for one career, these students will become obsolete as workers because of where technology is taking industry. We must re-educate our workforce in order for them to serve the changing business world.

> *Online learning trends develop because technologies and concepts fit the needs of an evolving population.*

The educational arena is focusing its energies on modifying curricula to bridge more of the changes and to reduce these re-educational requirements. This is being done by factoring more applied materials into the presentation of theories and focusing more heavily on critical thinking skills. This will help extend the value of initial educational objectives, but it will not fulfill the more specific needs of the organizations involved. While traditionally much of this need is fulfilled today by corporate educational functions, in the future this work will be subcontracted to specialists in various fields, or it will be offered outside the normal workplace situation. Online education is the logical choice to provide this capacity, whether through corporate educational programs or through colleges, universities, and specialized educational groups.

> *The challenge in delivering online learning is to solve problems in assimilating technologies into learning models*

If the prediction of five to seven career changes in a working lifetime is anywhere near accurate, a number of new alternatives will be required to meet the associated educational needs. Online programs will meet many of these needs. Schools such as the University of Phoenix and Baker College already offer multiple programs designed to meet these needs, and both are likely to add programs that are on the drawing board today to meet future needs.

Establishing a base for the future

It is interesting to watch the development of technological alternatives taking place today. In many cases, the drive for the technologies can be traced directly to the traditional classroom. Those driving the technologies often are from the classroom and find it appropriate to replicate the on-ground classroom in the online format.

While some value lies in this approach, some thought leaders in online programs are asking for a fresh approach to providing new technologies. They are asking for approaches that support facilitation processes that are common to online models, as opposed to the more common lecture models of the on-ground classroom educational models. The following table defines four of the major differences between on-ground and online models. These are generalized, and this list may differ among institutions, but this will provide you some comparative elements.

On-Ground Models	Online Models
lecture-driven activities highly structured discussions	discussion-driven activities lightly-structured discussions
faculty-driven	faculty-guided
scheduled class times with all present	students/facilitator meet in the VC any time

The tools required to use each of these models effectively are not necessarily the same for each model. In fact, the two models demand rather significant modifications to the tools used to achieve the learning objectives. The main differentiating factor is the facilitative versus the lecture-driven approaches to providing basic materials to students.

For example, the lecture-driven activities of the traditional classroom require the basics of a normal classroom setting. Students gather at one location, and normal classroom tools are present: a podium, a white board, perhaps a flip chart, and an overhead projector.

In the online model, students are distributed, and the instructor addresses them from a computer located virtually anywhere a telephone connection is available. Depending on the dynamics selected by the institution offering the course, the classroom process can be asynchronous, synchronous, or even a hybrid. The key is that it is very different than what is used in the on-ground classroom model.

If the person selecting the technology is from the on-ground tradition and has not been involved with online processes, they will try to use the familiar tools of the on-ground version in the online approach. They will want to be able to send voice and pictures. They may want to use e-mail to direct the presentation of lectures and discussions that result from the lectures. Control will be sought to assure that examinations are proctored and that the students on the other end of the technology are the individuals who registered for the class.

If the person selecting the technology is from the online community, they will quickly base their choice on a computer-based package, selected to meet the dialogue level planning for the program. This will be Convene, Embanet, or a similar product, depending on whether the program is to be Internet-based or store-and-forward in design. The need for audio and video would be analyzed carefully in terms of the needs of the online program and probably would not be incorporated.

Once technology decisions are appropriately directed to the online model, as opposed to adapting it to the on-ground model, we can look at where technologies are going in terms of our needs.

Technology directions

A number of technologies are available today that could be useful in the online paradigm. The availability of technology is well ahead of our ability to assimilate them into our learning models. Anticipate that this will be the case for years to come. Below is a partial list of reasons for this lag:

- *Costs*: The cost of many of the new technologies is high and difficult to justify on a cost-benefit basis.

- *Compatibility*: Students' systems are not always compatible with the technologies that are most desirable. For example, you might want to use CD-ROM programs; about 25% of the systems in use today have CD-ROM drives installed. While the cost of these devices is relatively low (about $200, including a sound board), many students' systems will not accept the upgrade or will require upgrading in other areas (software, memory, operating system, etc.) before a CD-ROM drive can be successfully installed. This is a serious problem and one that will require attention each time a group wants to move up the technological ladder.

- *Lack of strategic technology migration planning*: Along with the previous reason, incorporating new technology into curricula requires planning. Most institutions want to publish special equipment requirements of a course offering in the school's catalogue; they require the information long before students receive the catalogues. The usual lead time for catalogue information is about one year. This requirement cannot be met without strategic planning, and even if it is met, the cycle is too long to keep up with changes in technology.

- *Program design limitations*: The depth of many online program plans available today is not sufficient to provide a foundation for long-range technological planning, and the rate of change in available technologies adds to the difficulty of selecting any longer-term path of planning. As a result, many programs are implemented on a day-by-day, trial-and-error basis.

The real challenge is not the availability of technologies; the real challenge is solving the problems that prevent us from assimilating technologies into these learning models in a cost-effective way.

Watch these technologies

Following is a list of some of the most significant areas in which technologies of interest to the online educational community will be directed:

♦ *The Internet*: This will be the primary technology to watch. Many educational service providers are focused on using the Internet as a delivery vehicle, a research tool, a voice and video carrier, and an international means of linking knowledge resources such as libraries, special interest forums, and similar resources.

♦ *Special Internet options*: These will be offered to meet the utility grade requirements of education. These networks also will provide access to special capabilities such as audio feeds, video bandwidth, and interactive synchronized capabilities.

♦ *Hybrid technologies*: These include linking computers, cable services, telephone networks, and satellite links, which will provide attractive alternatives for receiving educational material in the home or in special facilities.

♦ *Computer hardware*: Special low cost hardware focused on receiving and handling educational offerings are being developed for the marketplace. Some will be supplied with specific programs installed for compatibility purposes.

- *Communications carriers*: Speed and reliability have long been limitations to the movement of large volumes of material between sources and students. This is being resolved through the creation of high-speed alternatives for moving files, programs, books, video ancillaries, and audio components. Cable, wireless telephone services, low cost desktop satellite access, and new compression software are contributing to making this option more viable.

The list can be expanded, but this offers an idea of where the emphasis is being focused. This should help you in developing your planning by showing you how to avoid roadblocks to your particular plan.

In summary

Online education is poised for great growth in the next decade. The resistance that was so long a roadblock to acceptance in traditional settings is evaporating as institutions begin to adopt online programs. Also, many of the primary technological issues are no longer a concern to the design and user communities. We can buy inexpensive workstations that are reliable and communications programs that are fast and cost-effective. This, together with the growing need for ways to distribute and receive educational programs that meet the needs of a changing environment, have provided a fertile environment for the expansion of online education with unprecedented speed.

Our technological requirements will be met and exceeded at the time we need it, or even before we can use it. As stated earlier in this chapter:

The real challenge is not the availability of technologies; the real challenge is solving the problems that prevent us from assimilating technologies into these learning models in a cost-effective way.

Index

V

W

Glossary of Terms

asynchronous - the absence of a timing requirement. For online learning purposes, the term asynchronous means that those participating in a given program are not required to be on a system or at a specific location at the same time.

bounded interactive - In terms of online educational processes, the bounded interactive model refers to an interactive learning model that utilizes structure and tools to limit dialog levels thus allowing the appropriate number of students to participate in an interactive online learning process.

CD-ROM - a compact disc containing data that can be read by a computer.

consultative - The term consultative, used in the online realm, refers to the manner in which the instructor/facilitator functions within the virtual classroom. The instructor /facilitator takes on the role of a consultant as the online learning model moves towards the independent study end of the learning continuum.

Convene, International - 250 Montgomery Street, San Francisco, CA 94104- a provider of online educational software that serves those providing online courses

curriculum - the courses offered by an educational institution and/or a set of courses constituting an area of specialization

cyber - a prefix, taken from the word cybernetics, used to describe a person, thing, or idea as part of the computer and information age

distance learning - Any formal approach to learning in which the majority of the instruction occurs while the educator and learner are at a distance from each other. Is used interchangeably with the term distance education. Distance education is defined, for the purposes of accreditation review, as a formal educational process in which the majority of the instruction occurs when student and instructor are not in the same place. Instruction may be synchronous or asynchronous. Distance education may employ correspondence study, or audio, video, or computer technologies.

Embanet Corporation, 308-20 Wynford Drive, Don Mills, Ontario, Canada M3C 1J4 - a provider of online educational software that serves those providing online courses.

facilitator - In the online context, a facilitator helps students to pursue the required knowledge, but relies on peer to peer efforts for a substantial amount of class discussion. Interactive and bounded interactive online learning models are structured to support a facilitated learning process.

HTML (Hypertext Markup Language) - the set of "markup" symbols or codes inserted in a file intended for display on a World Wide Web browser. The markup tells the Web browser how to display a Web page's words and images for the user.

HTTP (Hypertext Transfer Protocol) - the set of rules for exchanging files (text, graphic images, sound, video, and other multimedia files) on the World Wide Web. Relative to the TCP/IP suite of protocols (which are the basis for information exchange on the Internet), HTTP is an application protocol.

hybrid - a word used in the online world to indicate a 'mixing of', for example, a hybrid online course may involve both online and on-ground activities within a single learning process.

institutional readiness - an assessment of an entity's ability to support activities associated with online processes

interactive - mutually or reciprocally active; refers to an online learning process that requires a significant exchange of information between individuals participating in the learning process

Internet - often called simply "the Net," - a worldwide system of computer networks and, in a larger sense, the people using it. It was conceived by the Advanced Research Projects Agency (ARPA) of the U.S. government in 1969 and was called the ARPAnet. The Internet is now a public, cooperative and self-sustaining facility accessible worldwide. The most widely used part of the Internet is the World Wide Web.

Internet provider(IP) (also called Internet or independent service provider [ISP]) - a service company that provides individuals and other companies access to the Internet and other related services such as Web site building and serving

ISDN - Integrated Services Digital Network - a set of CCITT/ITU standards for digital transmission over ordinary telephone copper wire as well as over other media. ISDN requires adapters at both ends of the transmission so an access provider also needs an ISDN adapter. ISDN is generally available from your phone company in many urban areas in the United States and Europe.

learning continuum - a range of learning possibilities from pure Socratic method to independent study which contains all possible learning models.

learning outcome - the desirable end result of a given learning activity; there may be more than one per seminar.

learning paradigm - a set of structures, cultures, and processes that are typically associated with a given way of presenting education. The online learning paradigm has a given set of characteristics associated with it that are significantly different from those characteristics associated with learning processes that are understood to be traditional in nature.

mentorship - the use of a more experienced person supporting a less experienced person in some activity relating to the presenting of an online learning process.

models - a way of representing learning activity formats and/or structures utilized to present educational processes.

modem - a device that converts signals produced by one type of device (as a computer) to a form compatible with another (as a telephone).

MOO - an object-oriented MUD - According to Canton Becker, author of "The Unofficial Moo Guide Tutorial," a MOO is:"...just a programming language in which you design objects. Everything is an object. Rooms are objects, exits are objects, possessions are objects, even your MOO alter-ego/avatar is an object".

MUD - originally Multi-User Dungeon; now sometimes Multi-user Dimension - an inventively structured social experience on the Internet, managed by a computer program and often involving a loosely organized context or theme, such as a rambling old castle with many rooms or a period in national history. Some MUDs are ongoing adventure games; others are educational in purpose; and others are simply social.

on-ground - educational processes that are associated with activities that take place in a traditional setting, i.e., in a building, in a traditional classroom, not in a distance format.

online - being online refers to educational activities that take place while using a computer as the primary communication vehicle.

online service provider (OSP) - a company that provides access to the Internet through its own special user interface and proprietary services. The main OSPs are America Online (with, as of mid-1996, about 8 million users), Compuserve (5 million users), and Prodigy (2 million users). Connecting to the Internet through an OSP is an alternative to connecting through one of the national, regional, or local independent service providers (ISPs) or through a telecommunications company, such as AT&T or MCI.

platform - a software package that supports online educational processes.

server - a computer program that provides services to other computer programs in the same or other computers.

The computer that a server program runs in is also frequently referred to as a server (though it may contain a number of server and client programs). In the server/client programming model, a server is a program that awaits and fulfills requests from client programs in the same or other computers.

Socratic method - of or relating to Socrates, his followers, or his philosophical method of systematic doubt and questioning of another to elicit a clear expression of a truth supposed to be implicitly known by all rational beings; refers to the use of a learning process that utilizes the life, work, and educational experiences of the participants to produce a synergistic effect through a facilitator who guides the process to its intended outcomes.

store-and-forward - a process in which information is retained in the location generating the information (store),and is forwarded to one or more locations during a connection to a host system upon receiving a request for the information.

synchronous - happening, existing, or arising at precisely the same time. In the context of online teaching and learning, this is the use of procedures and technologies that require the student(s) and the facilitator be linked through a computer; all participants are required to be connected at the same time.

technology - a manner of accomplishing a task, especially using technical processes, methods, or knowledge.

text-based - refers to the utilization of text as the primary source for information exchange in supporting a given learning event.

tools - the utilization of processes, techniques, software, events, and other means of achieving a defined outcome.

virtual classroom (VC) - an area within a computer, created by a software program, that allows for educational processes to take place. A person attends a virtual classroom through a computer.

World Wide Web (WWW or the Web) - the universe of network-accessible information; all the resources and users on the Internet that are using the Hypertext Transport Protocol (HTTP), a method of instant cross-referencing. Web "surfing" is done with a Web browser. - *see also the Internet.*